Better Homes and Gardens®
STEP-BY-STEP
Kitchen
& Bath Projects

Better Homes and Gardens® Books
Des Moines, Iowa

Better Homes and Gardens® Books
An imprint of Meredith® Books

Step-by-Step Kitchen & Bath Projects
Editors: Benjamin W. Allen, Linda Hallam, Paula Marshall
Associate Art Director: Tom Wegner
Copy Editor: James Sanders
Proofreader: Deborah Morris Smith
Copy Chief: Catherine Hamrick
Copy and Production Editor: Terri Fredrickson
Electronic Production Coordinator: Paula Forest
Editorial and Design Assistants: Jennifer Norris, Karen Schirm, Kaye Chabot, Barbara A. Suk
Production Director: Douglas M. Johnston
Production Manager: Pam Kvitne
Assistant Prepress Manager: Marjorie J. Schenkelberg

Produced by Greenleaf Publishing, Inc.
Publishing Director: Dave Toht
Author: Steve Cory
Editorial Art Director: Jean DeVaty
Assistant Editor: Rebecca JonMichaels
Design: Melanie Lawson Design
Illustrations: Bob Stocki, Dick Ticcioni, Art Factory
Technical Consultants: Joseph Hansa, Charlie Havens

Cover Photograph: Tony Kubat Photography
Production and Back Cover Design: John Seid

Meredith® Books
Editor in Chief: James D. Blume
Design Director: Matt Strelecki
Managing Editor: Gregory H. Kayko
Executive Shelter Editor: Denise L. Caringer

Director, Sales & Marketing, Retail: Michael A. Peterson
Director, Sales & Marketing, Special Markets: Rita McMullen
Director, Sales & Marketing, Home & Garden Center Channel: Ray Wolf
Director, Operations: Valerie Wiese

Vice President, General Manager: Jamie L. Martin

Better Homes and Gardens® Magazine
Editor in Chief: Jean LemMon
Executive Building Editor: Joan McCloskey

Meredith Publishing Group
President, Publishing Group: Christopher Little
Vice President, Consumer Marketing & Development: Hal Oringer

Meredith Corporation
Chairman and Chief Executive Officer: William T. Kerr

Chairman of the Executive Committee: E. T. Meredith III

All of us at Better Homes and Gardens® Books are dedicated to providing you with information and ideas you need to enhance your home. We welcome your comments and suggestions about this book on kitchens and baths. Write to us at: Better Homes and Gardens® Books, Do-It-Yourself Editorial Department, 1716 Locust St., Des Moines, IA 50309–3023.

Note to the Reader: Due to differing conditions, tools, and individual skills, Meredith Corporation assumes no responsibility for any damages, injuries suffered, or losses incurred as a result of following the information published in this book. Before beginning any project, review the instructions carefully, and if any doubts or questions remain, consult local experts or authorities. Because local codes and regulations vary greatly, you always should check with local authorities to ensure that your project complies with all applicable local codes and regulations. Always read and observe all of the safety precautions provided by any tool or equipment manufacturer, and follow all accepted safety procedures.

TABLE OF CONTENTS

INTRODUCTION

Making-over a kitchen or a bath can range from replacing a sink and doing some painting to a major remodeling involving cabinets, fixtures, flooring, and lighting. Even if no walls are moved or windows removed or added, kitchen and bath remodelings are complicated, involving all the major systems of the home. Most people assume these jobs can be handled only by professionals with years of experience. Fear of the unknown drives homeowners to pay thousands of dollars to remodeling contractors to do jobs they could handle themselves. Today, homeowners have access to a wide range of kitchen and bath products, many of which have been designed with the do-it-yourselfer in mind

Step-by-Step Kitchen and Bath Projects explains how kitchens and baths are put together and gives you all the information you need to make most any improvement, be it major or minor. Perhaps best of all, *Step-by-Step Kitchen and Bath Projects* helps you evaluate which projects you can take on yourself. Doing the work yourself can be a budget-sparing and satisfying way to improve your home. But it is important to have a good idea how long the job will take; you may want to hire a professional just to save yourself the aggravation of being without a kitchen or bath for a month or so.

Working to Code

Although you are an amateur working on your own house, you have the same responsibilities as a licensed plumber, electrician, and carpenter. You must provide for a supply of pure and wholesome water and for the safe passage of liquids, solid wastes, and gases to the outside of your house. Any electrical installations you make must remain safe for decades. And any structures you build must be stable and sound. This means you must use only those techniques and materials that are acceptable to the building codes of your locality.

The procedures in this book represent the editors' understanding of the Uniform Plumbing Code (UPC) and the National Electrical Code (NEC). Local building codes are based on these, but can vary greatly from place to place. If there are no local codes covering the work you will be doing, consult the national codes. Ask your reference librarian to see the latest edition of the UPC or NEC. If local codes cover your project, they supersede any national requirements. (Canadian residents may obtain a copy of the Canadian National Plumbing Code by contacting Publication Sales M-20, National Research

Council of Canada, Ottawa, Ontario K1A 0R6. Phone number for Canadian residents is 1-800-672-7990. To obtain a copy of the Canadian Electrical Code, write the Canadian Standards Association, 178 Rexdale Boulevard, Etobicoke, Ontario M9W 1R3 or, within Canada, call 1-800-463-6726.

Working With Your Local Building Department

Always check with your local building department if you plan to extend an existing electrical circuit or add a new one or if you will be changing your plumbing in any substantial way. In addition, check local codes if you will be changing the structure of your house or if you think your existing wiring, plumbing, or structure may be substandard. Codes may seem bothersome, but they are designed to make your home safe and worry-free. Ignoring codes can lead to costly mistakes, health hazards, and even difficulties in selling your house someday.

Consult with your local building department and make arrangements for permits and inspections before you begin a project. Neglecting to do so could cause you the expense and trouble of tearing out and redoing your work.

There's no telling what kind of inspector you will get: He or she could be helpful, friendly, and flexible; or you might get a real stickler. But no matter what sort of personality you'll be dealing with, your work will go better if you follow these guidelines:

■ This book is a good place to start, but learn as much as you can about each project before you talk with an inspector from your local building department. That way, you'll be able to avoid miscommunication and get your permits more quickly. Your building department may have literature concerning your type of installation. If not, consult national codes.

■ Go to your building department with a plan to be approved or amended; don't expect the building department's inspectors to plan the job for you.

■ Present your plan with neatly drawn diagrams and a complete list of the materials you will be using.

■ Be sure you clearly understand when you need to have inspections made. Do not cover up any work that needs to be inspected.

■ Be as courteous as possible. Inspectors often are wary of homeowners. Show the inspector you are serious about doing things the right way and comply with any requirements put forth.

How to Use This Book

At the beginning of the Kitchen Improvements and Bathroom Improvements sections, you will find idea-filled color photos. Once you've decided on the projects you are going to tackle, refer to the pages that address your specific needs. If you plan on taking on a major remodeling project, you will find sections describing how to plan basic layouts and choose materials, as well as suggestions for construction strategies. It is important to decide in which order you need to do each step.

Next, turn to the section regarding specific projects. Read through it and note what you need to buy and how long you can expect to spend working on each installation. Make your plans accordingly.

Many projects require fundamental construction skills. The last section, Basic Skills and Materials, gives you background on wiring, plumbing, carpentry, and wall and floor treatments. For more detailed information on these topics, see the Better Homes and Gardens® books *Step-by-Step Wiring, Step-by-Step Plumbing,* and *Step-by-Step Basic Carpentry.*

Feature Boxes

In addition to basic instructions, you'll find plenty of tips throughout the book. For every project, a You'll Need box tells you about how long the project will take, what skills are necessary, and what tools you must have. The other tip boxes shown on this page provide practical help to ensure the work you do on your kitchen or bath will be as pleasurable as possible and that it will result in safe and long-lasting improvements to your home.

TOOLS TO USE

If you'll need special tools not commonly found in a home-owner's toolbox, we'll tell you about them in Tools to Use.

SAFETY

When a project in this book includes a potentially dangerous situation, we explain specific steps you can take to complete the job safely.

Money $ Saver

Throwing money at a job does not necessarily make it a better one. Money Saver offers smart ways to accurately estimate your material needs and make wise purchases.

MEASUREMENTS

Keep an eye out for this box when standard measurements or special measuring techniques are called for.

EXPERTS' INSIGHT

Tricks of the trade can make all the difference in helping you do a job quickly and well. Experts' Insight gives insiders' tips on how to make the job easier.

CAUTION!

When a how-to step requires special care, Caution! warns you what to watch out for. It will help keep you from doing damage to yourself or the job at hand.

KITCHEN REMODELING

A successful kitchen plan is a combination of style and practicality. When you're done, you'll want to love the feel and cherish the workability of your reformed kitchen. That's a tall order. Here's a collection of kitchens that succeed in both realms. Many of these have been done with a budget greater than your own, but that doesn't mean you can't achieve similar results. For example, the island shown at right doesn't have to be made by a professional. You can do it yourself with off-the-shelf cabinets (see pages 32–33). And by carefully choosing tile features, such as this kitchen's countertop edge and backsplash, and installing them yourself (see pages 39–41), you can achieve stunning style within a modest budget.

So soak in the good ideas shown on these pages and think creatively about how you might incorporate them into your design.

ABOVE: Set in a century-old home, this kitchen with its 12-foot ceilings and plenty of windows combines traditional style with contemporary function. The goal was to combine timeless style with up-to-date efficiency. *Tile, crown molding, and deep paneled cabinet doors set a traditional theme. Ample refrigerator space, a generous cooktop, and an eat-in island make it work for today.*

LEFT: Without much space to work with, this kitchen manages an ample work area and a distinctive style. A deep island adds generous counter space and successfully detours traffic away from the work core. Everything is at hand: dishwasher, sink, and cooktop. (The refrigerator is out of the photograph to the left of the sink.)

Style is established with distinctive light fixtures and a stunning tile backsplash, two ideas within the reach of most budgets and easily added to any kitchen. The homeowners painted the walls with a single coat of oil-base glaze, mixed with a combination of yellow and sienna artist's oils. They applied a second coat that contained more sienna than the first, then blotted it with paper towels.

ABOVE: *Before remodeling, this modest 12x14-foot kitchen suffered from flimsy metal cabinets and a clumsy layout that routed traffic through the middle of the work area. To make the most of the space available, a new peninsula was added, doubling the kitchen's counter space and moving traffic away from the work area. The homeowner removed soffits to eliminate a brooding feel to the room. Gloom also was conquered by a well-conceived combination of downlights, hanging fixtures, and undercabinet lighting. Are granite countertops outside your budget? Consider granite-patterned laminate.*

LEFT and **BELOW:** *Let's face it: Cooking requires time at the sink. To make the best of the situation, the window in this kitchen was replaced with a bay window for plenty of light, an enhanced view, and a place for plenty of plants. You can achieve the same effect at less cost with a garden window (see page 51).*

LEFT: *Before this kitchen was made over, it suffered from an earlier case of too much remodeling. As with so many kitchens, nearly as much work went into demolition as new construction. Soffits covered the top 12 inches of the kitchen windows, and a dropped ceiling cancelled the generosity of the 9½-foot-high ceiling. All the surfaces had to be replaced: floors, ceiling, walls, and countertops. Old cabinets were refinished and repositioned; a new island has cubbyholes in both sides, eating space, and storage for pans under the cooktop.*

BELOW: *Once you've settled on the ideal layout for your kitchen, plan for maximum decorating flexibility in the future. In this kitchen, having plain white cabinets and no soffit allows plenty of open wall space for wallcovering and places for colorful collectibles. This room is ready for whatever palette of colors the future brings, whether it be with this homeowner or another.*

ABOVE: *Light and space are important kitchen considerations. This compact sink area maximizes overhead storage space with short, soffitlike cabinets. Beneath them, downlights provide generous illumination for the sink preparation area. The crisp and clean look of the cabinets and countertops suits almost any architectural style.*

LEFT: *Makeovers don't have to be drastic. Appliances and basic hookups didn't move in this eat-in kitchen, but the cabinets got a facelift with new maple cabinet frames and blue laminate panels. The same blue is echoed in a band of trim above the cabinets and on the exterior door and window trim. Well-planned task and general lighting and handsome fixtures keep the kitchen bright, making work easy and pleasant.*

CHOOSING KITCHEN MATERIALS

A wide range of materials can be used in a kitchen, regardless of the style and layout you select. Looks, cost, and utility are the considerations. Unless you have an unlimited budget, therein lies the stuff of compromise.

Oddly enough, more expensive materials often require more maintenance. For example, butcher block and other hardwood countertops need frequent oiling to look their best. Even granite can stain in ways laminate will not.

But some expensive touches can provide just the boost a kitchen needs: a stained glass front to a cabinet door, a tile border, or a decorative light fixture.

Think in terms of contrast. Hardwood floors combined with wood cabinets may be overkill. White cabinets with white countertops may look antiseptic. Pack some punch into your design by using materials that complement each other.

It's a newly remodeled kitchen, but comforting tile countertops make this remodeling look like it's been around for a long time. Wall tiles running from the countertop to the cabinets give the impression that this is a serious cook's kitchen, ready for hard work. Light colors enlarge the room.

Wood can bring a warm glow to your kitchen. Besides being affordable and easy to clean, laminate counters don't fight the appealing beauty of wood cabinets. Underfoot, vinyl flooring cut in geometric patterns imitates vintage floorcloths.

Plan the right material in the right place. Grout can stain over the years. If you want tile without the hassle of intensive cleaning, use it on the backsplash as an appealing accent, then use a low-maintenance material for the countertop.

ABOVE: *You can keep the best of your old kitchen. Marred by water and burn stains, these butcher-block countertops almost were given up for lost. Sanding and refinishing renewed them. Painting the old wood cabinets lets the countertops shine as a feature of the kitchen. Such salvaging left room in the budget for eye-catching decorative tile used to replace a dated, brick veneer backsplash.*

LEFT: *For each material, there is a function. In this carefully planned kitchen makeover various materials were used to best advantage. Solid-surface countertops are used where the work is most intensive. On the informal eating area of the island, wood makes sense. By the same token, tile covers the floor near the sink and hardwood flooring is used where spills and overspray are less likely and cleanup less intensive.*

PLANNING A KITCHEN

Before you tackle questions of style, materials, and the specific features and appliances you might want to add to your kitchen, assess your needs:

■ *Storage space.* Make a list of the items you use often and those you seldom use. Plan a cabinetry layout that puts often-used items within easy reach.

■ *Counter space.* Consider how much space you need and where to best locate it. A cutting area near the sink or the garbage container, for instance, is helpful.

■ *Traffic flow.* Keep the traffic between the back door and the rest of the house away from the food preparation area. Design in a permanent detour. Also, if there's a bottleneck between the dining area and the sink, doing the dishes for a large dinner will be difficult and take the fun out of entertaining.

■ *Lighting.* Kitchen lighting should be bright, but not glaring. In most cases, a combination of overhead, hanging, and undercabinet lighting makes for the best arrangement (see page 13).

■ *Eating area.* Even if you usually do not eat meals in the kitchen, having a spot for a couple of kids to snack or for guests to talk with the cook makes the kitchen a friendlier place. Islands or peninsulas work well as informal eating areas (see page 32–33).

When it comes time to draw your plans, a great many resources are at your disposal. Home centers, cabinetmakers, and kitchen specialty stores often have computer programs that show you how various configurations will look in your kitchen. Many also give you an instant quote on what the proposed kitchen would cost. But beware: These suppliers may insist that you buy their products and/or use their contractors, which could mean extra expense. If you have a home computer, inexpensive kitchen-planning programs are available; many of these work just as well as those offered by stores.

For a low-tech option, purchase a set of kitchen design templates. With these scale-drawn cutouts of cabinets and appliances, you can move the pieces around until you find the right configuration for your situation.

Expect to try many design ideas before you hit on the one that best suits your needs, space limitations, and budget. Compromise is inevitable. Expect to spend lots of time choosing materials and appliances. Talk to people whose kitchens you like. Gather ideas from books and magazines. And visit home centers and appliance stores for a firsthand look.

Use comfortable dimensions.
Plan countertops so you can reach items easily. The dimensions shown at left are the most comfortable for average-size adults. Tables should be 29 to 31 inches high if you will be sitting on chairs, slightly higher if you will be using stools. A 34-inch-high surface can be used as both a counter and a table.

Base cabinets and counters rarely vary in height, but wall cabinets range from 30 to 42 inches in height. Unless you are a tall person, the top shelf of a 42-inch-high wall cabinet will not be accessible without a boost up.

Always keep appliance doors in mind. Will you be able to walk through the space while the dishwasher or oven door is open?

Although it may be tempting to design a kitchen around children, remember they grow up, and a step stool can take care of most of their problems.

Keep items within comfortable reach.

Eye level should determine window height.

Often-used items go here.

18" between counter tops and bottom of wall cabinets

36" countertop height

24" minimum clearance over sinks and ranges

shoulder height

Use upper shelves for heavy items.

Rarely used items go here.

There should be a minimum of 40 inches between cabinets; 48 inches between appliances. If cabinet doors and appliances face each other, plan for the space needed to open doors.

Plan a complete lighting system.
Effective kitchen lighting uses several sources, with different light switches so you can vary the lighting according to your needs. Adjustable track lighting and dimmer switches further increase your options.

In this kitchen, recessed can lighting provides general illumination. Overhead track lights can be swiveled to highlight display shelves and artwork—anything you wish to dramatize. The suspended fixture can be switched on during meals. While doing the dishes, two small recessed lights are handy. And undercabinet lighting is essential for working on counter surfaces; your body will shadow all of the other lights.

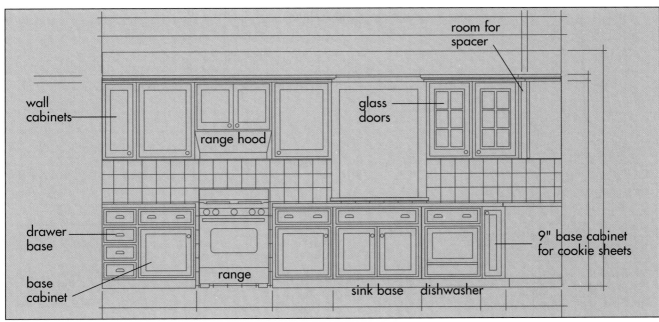

Make elevation drawings.
Whether you're using a computer program or making a drawing to scale on graph paper, take the time to make elevation drawings. This step helps you avoid costly mistakes. In a kitchen, an error of 1 inch or less can be a disaster, especially when expensive cabinets and appliances are involved.

Avoid base cabinet doors wider than 20 inches and wall cabinet doors wider than 18 inches; both stick out awkwardly when open.

Although you may want to fit in as many items as possible, don't squeeze too tightly—remember that few walls are perfectly plumb or square. Allow an extra ½ inch of space on either side of ranges and refrigerators. Plan on putting in small spacers at the ends of cabinet runs to provide a buffer against wall variations.

Some kitchen designers develop plans so the wall and base cabinet doors align vertically. However, unless your kitchen is large, such symmetry seldom is noticeable.

CHANGING FLOOR PLANS

Here are five real-life situations where the utility of the kitchen was improved dramatically. As you study these and set about planning your own kitchen, keep in mind that each decision to move walls increases the complexity and expense of your project. Not only will demolition be a big mess, but plumbing and wiring nightmares may lurk in those walls. Still, it often is worthwhile to move a wall to achieve the ideal kitchen layout.

Before you plan on removing walls, check to see if they are load bearing, ones that provide structural support for the upper floors of your house. Consult with a professional if you are not sure. If you do remove a load-bearing wall, you must support the ceiling temporarily while you work, then install a beam strong enough to carry the load.

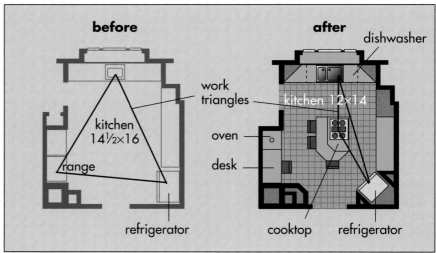

Add an island.
This large kitchen was not used to full advantage. The work triangle between the range, refrigerator, and sink was too large. And traffic ran through the triangle.

Although a bit smaller, the new kitchen functions more efficiently.

A new island equipped with a cooktop tightens the work triangle and provides needed storage space and an eating area. The less-used oven is to one side of the traffic area. The sink, with its window view, remains in its original place to avoid costly plumbing changes.

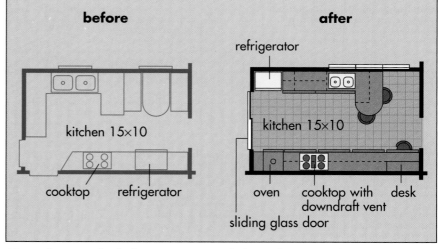

Move doors and windows.
This kitchen had three doorways, wasting valuable wall space. The refrigerator was located inconveniently in the traffic path. The fixed benches in the eating nook were uncomfortable and used up a lot of space. Two small windows kept the space gloomy.

In the remodeled kitchen, sliding glass doors let in plenty of light and improved the view. Moving the sink allowed room for the refrigerator. Replacing the range with a cooktop made for a more efficient work triangle. The wall oven, which is used less often, doesn't interfere with the main work area. Chairs around the new peninsula are more comfortable than the fixed benches of the old eating area.

Incorporate a mud room.

This original kitchen was cramped and had no natural light. Like many older kitchens, it lacked counter space. The mud room walls were removed, and a weathertight entry door was installed, along with a small porch outside. This made room for a small laundry area. Relocating the doorway improved traffic flow. A new closet has a short wall that makes the refrigerator appear built in. The new peninsula runs through the middle of the kitchen, separating the work area from the traffic flow and providing counter and dining space.

Capture entryway space.

Before renovation, traffic went straight through the kitchen to reach the back door. Neither the cooktop nor the refrigerator had any nearby counter space, and there was no eating space. The solution: Sacrifice the laundry room and rework the entry to provide an alternate route outside, cutting down on traffic through the kitchen. A bump-out window over the sink makes the narrow space seem larger. New countertops next to the range add much-needed counter space and makes the kitchen more useable.

Open things up.

Neither this kitchen nor the nearby dining room were large enough to function as they should. The homeowners chose to unlock existing space by removing the wall between the two rooms and taking space from an adjoining room.

With the wall removed, there is space for a peninsula, providing much-needed counter space. Moving the door reroutes traffic away from the work triangle. A built-in buffet provides storage for tableware as well as a serving counter for entertaining.

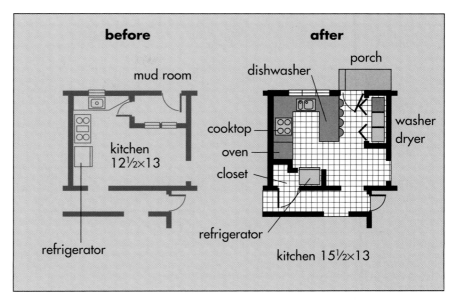

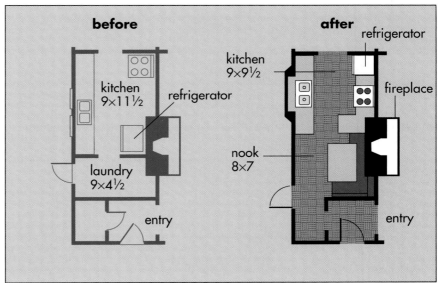

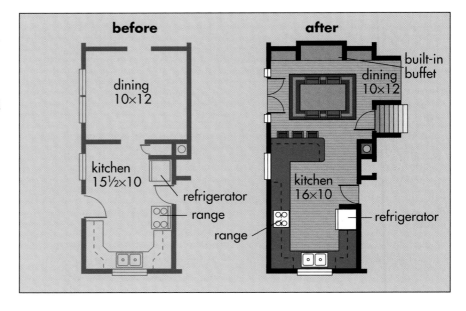

PLANNING YOUR CONSTRUCTION STRATEGY

A kitchen renovation is the most disruptive home improvement of all. No matter how cool-headed a person you may be or how harmonious your family life, a month or more of being without a kitchen will take its toll.

Kitchen remodelings are notorious for taking longer than expected. Often, cabinets and appliances don't arrive on time or have to be returned because of defects or a misorder. Even if the major installations go smoothly, the details at the end of the job can take a surprisingly long time to complete.

So plan carefully to avoid snags. Make sure everything is ordered well ahead of time. Be as certain as possible of your choices because changes in plans or materials will slow things down dramatically. And take special care to do things in the most logical order (see chart, *above right*).

If you plan on doing the work yourself, set aside some vacation time for the project. Working only weekends and evenings simply prolongs the misery. If you hire a professional contractor for all or part of the work, be sure to agree to a firm schedule with monetary penalties should the job take longer than promised.

Most of the individual operations involved in a kitchen remodeling are within reach of homeowners with some do-it-yourself experience. But be aware that a wide range of construction skills are involved: electrical, plumbing, tiling, carpentry—even specialized skills like installing granite slabs. If you are not confident of your ability in any of these areas, consult the basic skills section on pages 86–107.

SCHEDULING CONSTRUCTION

No two kitchen makeovers are exactly alike, but here is a plan of attack to suit most situations:

■ *Demolition.* Cover scratchable surfaces. Completely tear out all walls and remove debris.

■ *Rough wiring.* Install all new circuits and boxes and run all the cables.

■ *Vents.* Cut any needed holes for exhaust fans.

■ *Rough plumbing.* Install and test all supply lines, shutoff valves, and drain/vent lines.

■ *Wall patching and priming.* Prepare all surfaces that won't be covered by permanent cabinets.

■ *Flooring.* Install new flooring, and cover it if it is scratchable. (If you are using expensive materials, you may want to install your flooring after installing the cabinets.)

■ *Cabinets.* Level and plumb, attach firmly to walls, and cover to keep from scratching.

■ *Painting and wallcovering.* Finish the walls and allow for plenty of drying time.

■ *Countertop and backsplash.* Scribe and install.

■ *Finish electrical.* Install receptacles and light fixtures.

■ *Finish plumbing.* Install sinks, faucets, and dishwasher.

■ *Appliances.* Install ovens and cooktops; slide the range and refrigerator into place.

■ *Touch-ups.* Expect plenty of details to correct and complete.

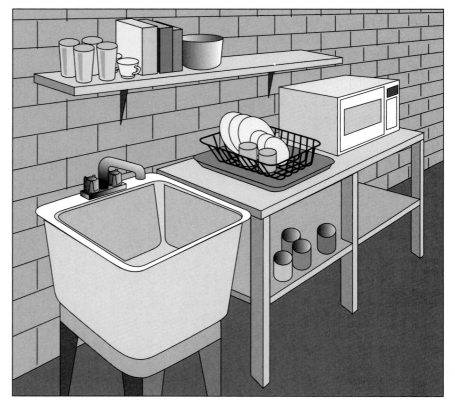

Set up a temporary kitchen.
With a laundry tub, microwave, and some temporary shelves, you can keep cooking while the sawdust flies. Some homeowners install a temporary galley kitchen in the family room before a major kitchen remodeling.

PAINTING CABINETS

Here's an inexpensive way to make a big difference in the appearance of your kitchen. If doors and drawer faces are in reasonable shape, a coat of paint can renew them. However, be aware that painting cabinetry correctly is a painstaking job. If you merely slap on the paint, the cabinets will look worse than when you started.

Decide how much of the cabinets you will paint. Usually, you need to paint only the stiles (the framing pieces), the drawer faces, and one side of the doors. You may want to paint the back side of the doors and the insides of the cabinets. (Cover the bottoms of shelves and drawers with shelf paper.) Choose a high-quality acrylic paint made for woodwork. Decide on the texture you like best. Use a roller for large areas. Allow paint plenty of time to dry before handling. When done, you'll have a surface that is almost as washable as laminate.

YOU'LL NEED

TIME: 2 days for an average-size kitchen.
SKILLS: Accurate painting.
TOOLS: Scrapers, sanding block, screwdriver, paintbrush, roller.

Money $ Saver

CHANGE THE HARDWARE

New hinges and door and drawer pulls are the ideal finishing touches to freshen up old cabinets. Select hardware before painting because you may have to fill in the holes in the cabinets if the new hardware fastens on differently.

1. Fill, sand, and prime.
Examine surfaces carefully for cracks and holes; paint will not cover any imperfections. Scrape and sand down high spots and fill scratch marks and cavities with wood putty. If you will be changing the location of pulls or knobs, fill the old screw holes. Sand filler smooth. Prime old enamel surfaces with an alkyd-based primer.

2. Paint doors and drawer faces.
Remove every piece of hardware—hinges and knobs or pulls—and set the doors and drawers on drop cloths. Support them with blocks of wood so no painted surface comes in contact with the drop cloths. Paint large areas with a roller and use a brush to touch up hard-to-get-to areas.

3. Strip hardware.
If you will be reusing the old hardware, clean it by soaking it overnight in paint remover. Buff lightly with steel wool or rub it with metal polish—the kind that leaves a protective film.

4. Paint the stiles.
Cover the countertop and other surfaces with masking tape as needed. Paint the framing pieces with long, smooth strokes. Begin at the least accessible points and work outward. Paint the inner surfaces, then work toward the outer surfaces.

STENCILING CABINETS

Once cabinets are painted, you can add decorative detail with stenciled designs. A variety of stencils are available, some quite complex. The safest approach is to use a small accent, rather than a dominating presence.

If your cabinets are covered with oil-based enamel paint, the stencils will not adhere properly. Prime and paint the cabinet surfaces before beginning.

YOU'LL NEED
TIME: About 1 day for a medium-size kitchen.
SKILLS: Marking level lines, laying out stencils.
TOOLS: Stenciling brush, straightedge, stencils, pencil.

Money $ Saver

REPLACING DOORS?
If your cabinets are too far gone to be improved by painting, you may want to replace the doors. Here are some tips to keep in mind:

■ Check prices. Many companies charge almost as much for doors as for entire cabinets. Often you can cut costs by ordering unfinished doors. Glass doors are expensive.

■ If the sides of cabinets are exposed, you may need to purchase sheets of veneer to match the new doors. Affix them with contact cement.

■ When ordering, provide a diagram showing the location of all doors and the exact sizes of the openings. Measure from stile to stile. Make sure the hinges and stiles of the new doors will match up when you install them.

1. Lay out the pattern.
You can do the stenciling with the doors on or off, whichever is most convenient. Using a straightedge and ruler, mark the boundaries with a light pencil line. Position the accent figures so they are spaced evenly along the length of the cabinets.

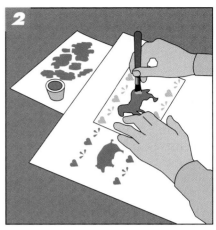

2. Apply the paint.
Attach the stencil in place firmly. Dip the stenciling brush in paint, then blot it on a paper towel until it is nearly dry. Apply the paint to the stencil with a firm, tapping motion. With practice, you can shade the figures to give them depth and dimension.

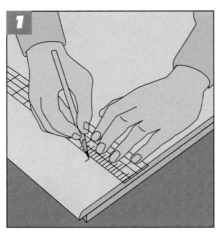

3. Remove the stencil.
Allow the paint to dry a bit, then carefully peel back the stencil. Don't slide the stencil as you remove it or you will smear the paint. Borders and additional small designs may be applied by using stamps or by hand-painting.

EXPERTS' INSIGHT

STENCILING TECHNIQUES
■ Purchase ready-made stencils in the design of your choice, or cut out your own design using blank sheets. Both are available at craft centers.

■ A sponge brush makes the work go quicker, but you won't get the subtle shadings that you can get with a stenciling brush.

■ If you have never stenciled before, it is a good idea to spend some time practicing. After you have repeated the process several times, you'll develop the technique that produces the most pleasing results—perhaps a lighter touch or an uneven, rather than a consistent, application may suit your tastes best.

SURFACING CABINETS WITH LAMINATE

If you have better-than-average carpentry skills and like the look of smooth laminate, this technique can give your cabinets a new lease on life. Surfacing with laminate is time-consuming, but the resulting surface is durable and easy to maintain. Laminate is relatively expensive, so plan your use of material before buying. Measure each piece needed. Work out a cutting plan, making sure each piece is an inch longer in both directions than the surface it will cover. Laminate comes in a variety of sizes; 20×30 inches, and 4×4-, 4×5- and 4×8-foot sheets.

YOU'LL NEED

TIME: Several days for an average-size kitchen.
SKILLS: Cutting with a power saw, spreading contact cement evenly, trimming laminate with a router.
TOOLS: Circular saw or tablesaw, rasp or hand file, sanding block, laminate trimmer or router with laminate-edging bit.

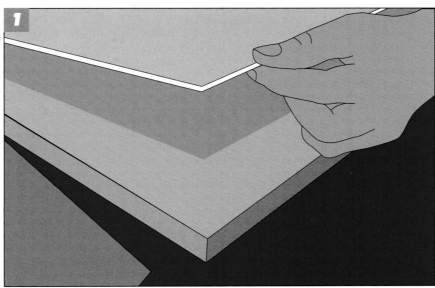

1. Glue laminate to doors.

Cut pieces of laminate that are at least ¼ inch, but not more than 1 inch, longer in both directions than the piece to be covered. In a dust-free room, apply contact cement evenly to the cabinet surface and to the back of the laminate piece.

After the cement is dry, carefully place the laminate on the surface to be covered so it overhangs all edges. Work carefully because once it is in place, it cannot be moved. You may want to place a piece of waxed paper on the surface, then position the laminate on top of the wax paper. Once the material is aligned correctly, pull out the paper. When the face piece is in place, cut and attach the edging strips.

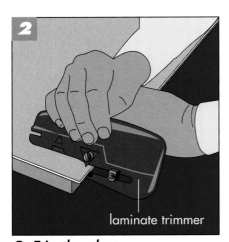

laminate trimmer

2. Trim the edges.

Use a laminate trimmer, as shown, to score a line for the final cut. Snap off the waste and smooth the edge with a hand file or a sanding block. For a more professional result, trim the edge using a router with a laminate-trimming bit.

laminate edging

CONTACT CEMENT

3. Surface the stiles.

Sand the stiles so the cement will adhere well. Cut oversized pieces, brush both stiles and the backs of the laminate with contact cement, and apply the pieces—first to the faces of the stiles and then to each of the sides.

hand file

4. Trim the edges.

Trim with a laminate trimmer or router, as you did with the door faces. Smooth the edge with a file. If you use a router you also will need a file to trim into the corners. Sand all the edges with fine sandpaper.

INSTALLING A RANGE HOOD

Providing a hole to vent a range hood can be a big job, especially if you have an old house with double brick construction. For a frame house, it may only take 1 or 2 hours. Running vent duct is straightforward: Connect the vent pieces together with screws and seal each joint with duct tape.

Don't vent a range hood into an attic or a crawl space; the grease it emits creates a fire hazard. Vent it outside. If that is not practical, purchase a ductless hood that captures grease in washable filters. Ductless hoods, however, will not get rid of heat, moisture, or odor.

YOU'LL NEED

TIME: 1 to 2 hours to a full day, depending on how difficult it is to cut the hole.
SKILLS: Basic carpentry skills; making electrical connections.
TOOLS: Drill, sabersaw, tin snips, screwdriver; other tools depending on wall construction.

BUY THE RIGHT SIZE FAN

■ Vent fans are rated according to the cubic feet of air per minute (cfm) they can move. There are many variables to take into account when figuring how powerful a fan you require. Your supplier will have the information you need.
■ If you need to vent spattering grease, you will need a strong fan otherwise only smoke, heat, and odor will be drawn out. The longer the vent, the stronger your fan needs to be; a flexible duct is less efficient than a smooth duct. The larger the fan, the larger diameter the vent duct should be.

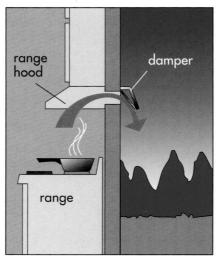

Venting out the wall.
This is the easiest and most common way to vent a range hood. Use the template supplied by the manufacturer to locate the hole. Cut the hole with a sabersaw for wood, or use a drill with a masonry bit and a cold chisel if you have to go cut through brick. The damper keeps drafts from coming in the house.

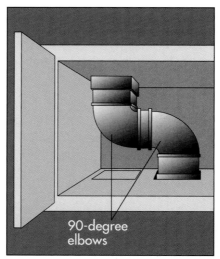

Using an existing duct.
If there is an existing duct, but it's located in the wrong place, you may be able to connect to it by using elbows. Cover the old hole, so the cabinet will be usable. Take extra care to seal the ductwork here, so grease does not leak into the cabinet.

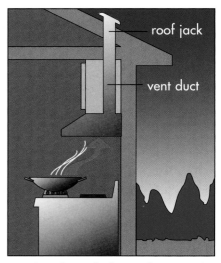

Venting through the roof.
If you cannot go through the wall, the roof may be your best option. (For greatest efficiency, choose the shortest route to the outside.) Run the duct through the cabinet above, then cut holes in the attic and the roof. Install a roof jack and be sure to use flashing so the roof does not leak.

Installing a downdraft vent.
If your cooktop or range is built into an island or peninsula, you can buy a large vent that comes down from the ceiling or get a cooktop with a built-in downdraft vent. The ductwork runs down through the floor to the outside.

CHOOSING CABINETS

Cabinets are the most visible elements in most kitchens and likely the biggest investment you'll make in your kitchen. Scan books and magazines and visit home centers and kitchen design shops to settle on the style of cabinets you want. Then you'll need to put together the configuration of cabinets that best suits your needs.

Measure your walls carefully before figuring which size cabinets you will need. See page 13 for a sample layout and examine the options shown on pages 23–27.

Some inexpensive cabinets, which you finish or paint yourself, are just as durable as more expensive units. Others are built shoddily. Make sure the frames and doors are square and check that no screws are driven into particleboard—they'll come out if the door is bumped and never again will attach firmly.

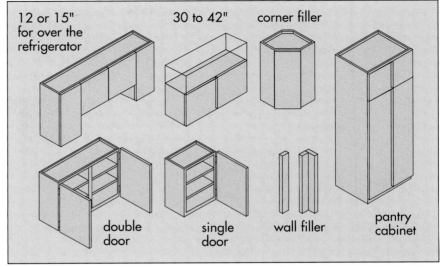

Selecting wall cabinets.
For the majority of wall cabinets, choose the most comfortable height—from 30 to 42 inches. Over the refrigerator, use a 12- or 15-inch cabinet (measure carefully) or just leave the space open and put stuff on top of the fridge. For inside corners, purchase a special corner cabinet and put a lazy Susan in it for the most efficient use of space. A tall pantry cabinet can store plenty of canned goods or can be used as a broom closet. Some wall cabinets can be installed upside-down to reverse the direction the doors open; if yours don't work this way, be sure to specify which side you want the hinges on.

EXPERTS' INSIGHT

HOW MUCH CABINETRY?
The best way to plan for cabinets is to catalog your dinnerware, utensils, and small appliances and designate storage for them as you choose cabinets. In general, keep the following guidelines in mind:

■ In a moderate-size kitchen (150 square feet or less), you should have at least 13 lineal feet of base cabinets and 12 lineal feet of wall cabinets.

■ A larger kitchen should have at least 16 feet of base cabinets and 15½ feet of wall cabinets.

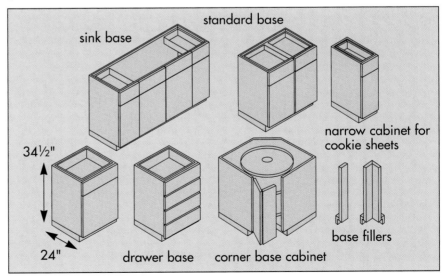

Selecting base cabinets.
Base cabinets generally come 34½ inches high by 24 inches deep to accommodate a countertop height of 36 inches and depth of 25 inches. For places where you need a shallower base cabinet and counter, you may be able to use a wall cabinet set on a 1×4 for a toe space. Most base cabinets have one drawer unit on top and storage shelves with doors below, but you may want at least one full drawer base. Check that the sink base you choose has an opening large enough for your sink.

BUYING CABINETS: STOCK OR CUSTOM?

■ Most major cabinet manufacturers have catalogs listing the cabinet types and amenities they produce. Sizes generally range from 9 to 48 inches in width, in 3-inch increments. There are a limited number of finishes and colors to choose from.

■ Watch prices carefully. Although stock cabinets are mass produced, some brands cost almost as much as custom cabinets. Basic cabinets often are reasonably priced, but prices climb on special cabinet inserts and amenities.

■ Ready-to-assemble or unfinished cabinets are often your least-expensive option. You can find these stacked on large shelves in home centers. They take some time to assemble and/or finish, but may be worth the trouble. Be sure you can purchase fillers, wire racks, and other amenities made to fit the cabinets. Before finally selecting the stain or finish for unfinished cabinets, test it on pieces of the same type wood.

■ Semicustom cabinets are built to your exact specifications by the manufacturer. This means that you can get cabinets that fit your spaces exactly and are finished in your choice of finish. However, they may be as limited in style options as stock cabinets. Also, these types of cabinets often take weeks or months to arrive. If the manufacturer makes a mistake, it could be weeks more before you finally have your cabinets.

■ Custom cabinets generally are the most expensive. They are measured on site by the fabricator and made locally, which might mean less of a wait compared with semicustom cabinets. Depending on the cabinetmaker, you also may have a larger selection of finishes and styles from which to choose. And if you need special cabinetry for an awkward place, a cabinetmaker can build it along with the rest of the cabinets.

FRAMED OR FRAMELESS?

You can distinguish the two basic methods of cabinet construction easily. Frameless cabinets, also called Euro-style or full-overlay cabinets, have only a thin space between drawers and drawer faces. Framed cabinets have stiles, or frame pieces, that are wider than the thickness of the cabinet walls. Because of this, the exposed edges of the cabinet frame pieces, called the reveal, are wider than those of frameless cabinets.

Frameless cabinets offer a cleaner, simpler look that often

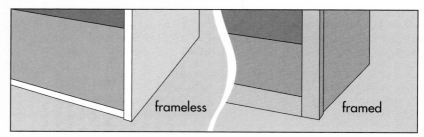

melds well with appliance fronts. With no frame in the way, they are a bit more efficient in their use of space. However, in corners, you will have to use spacers to allow the doors to open up completely.

Framed cabinets have a more traditional appearance, are stronger overall, and are easier to install. The disadvantage is that door and drawer openings, as well as roll-out accessories, are a bit smaller than with frameless cabinets. That means a less efficient use of space.

CHOOSING CABINET MATERIALS

Take a close look at the material from which the cabinets are made. Solid wood is used for cabinet frames, sometimes for doors, but rarely for the main body. Often cabinets are made of a combination of the following materials:

■ Particleboard, made by bonding wood fiber with resin, should be viewed with caution. If the material is not reinforced well with solid materials, it won't be strong. Long particleboard shelves sag over time. High quality particleboard, rated as 45-pound commercial grade, is better than standard particleboard. But no particleboard holds screws well.

■ Medium-density fiberboard has a harder surface than particleboard and accepts paint more readily. But it is no stronger than particleboard. Hinges should not be attached directly to it.

■ Laminates vary in quality. Standard plastic laminates, such as those used on countertops, are strong. Other products, such as melamine, are chipped easily. All laminates are difficult to repair.

■ Plywood, made by laminating thin layers (plies) of wood together, is the best material for structural support. It is strong, is almost impossible to crack, and accepts finishes well.

ADDING PULL-OUTS AND RACKS

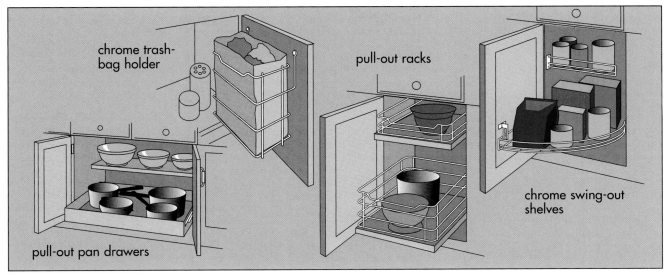

chrome trash-bag holder

pull-out racks

pull-out pan drawers

chrome swing-out shelves

Here's the quickest way to make your storage spaces more efficient and to add more useable space as well. Many cabinet areas, especially in base cabinets or on high shelves in wall cabinets, are hard to get at. It makes sense to add a storage rack directly on the door. A trash-bag holder frees up floor or base cabinet space your garbage container takes up. Large pull-out drawers make it much easier to get at pots, pans, and small appliances. With swing-out shelves, canned goods no longer are unreachable and forgotten in the depths of a cabinet.

REPLACING DRAWER GLIDES

Sticky or clunky-feeling drawers sometimes can be turned into smooth operators by taking the drawer out and cleaning or lubricating the parts. But some drawers may have been built with substandard glides, and others might have damaged glides. In either case, replace the type that has a single runner in the middle of the drawer with the type of glides shown at right.

YOU'LL NEED

TIME: About 1 hour.
SKILLS: Measuring, assembly, driving screws.
TOOLS: Drill with screwdriver bit and/or screwdriver, torpedo level.

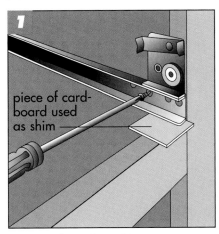

piece of cardboard used as shim

1. Attach to the cabinet.
You may need to attach a filler strip to the cabinet side so there is something into which you can screw the glide. Position the piece so it is raised slightly above the framing piece by using a thin shim. Drive the screws into the cabinet frame, level it with a torpedo level, and attach the other end with screws.

2. Attach to the drawer.
Position the drawer part of the glide so the front of it butts against the back of the drawer face and the flange on the other end aligns with the bottom of the side of the drawer. Secure the flanged end with screws. Move the front end up or down so it is parallel with the bottom of the drawer and attach with screws.

CHOOSING CABINET AMENITIES

Just as a bedroom closet can become more efficient when you organize it with shelves and rods, so your kitchen cabinets can work harder for you if you install the right equipment. A standard shelf holds items well enough, but all too often the cans and bottles in the back are hard to reach. It's bad enough with 12-inch-deep wall cabinets, but base cabinets, twice as deep, are even worse. Here are some cabinet amenities designed to make the most of otherwise wasted space.

When shopping for these items, look for amenities made from materials easy to keep clean. Wire racks rarely need more than a quick wipe. Plastic inserts often can be removed and washed. However, most flat surfaces need to be covered with scrubbable shelf paper.

A lazy Susan is a favorite cabinet insert choice. Not only does it make it easier to get at things in a wall cabinet, it uses inaccessible space deep in corner base cabinets.

All base cabinets have a few inches of space beneath them. Put that wasted space to use with a toe-space drawer. It slides out to hold canned goods, recyclables, a small step ladder, paper bags, and soda purchased by the case.

Sometimes simple organizers do the job. Drawer racks make it easy to find and store away spices.

For a standard base cabinet, consider combining racks on the doors with a swing-out rack system inside the cabinet. When installing racks on doors, make sure the door hinges are strong enough to support the weight of the items that will be stored on the racks. Small shelves, capable of holding only 12-ounce cans, may be a prudent choice.

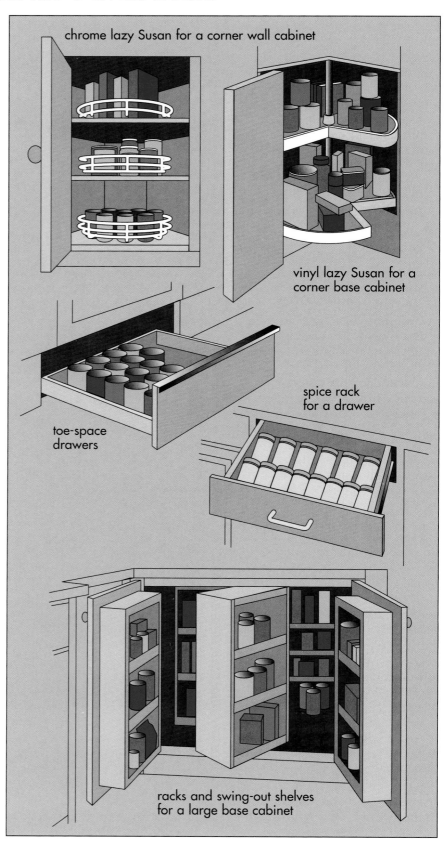

chrome lazy Susan for a corner wall cabinet

vinyl lazy Susan for a corner base cabinet

toe-space drawers

spice rack for a drawer

racks and swing-out shelves for a large base cabinet

If you have a heavy kitchen appliance that you use a lot but don't want on display, an appliance garage is the solution. Just roll up the door and you're ready to use it.

One amenity that tames unruly stacks of pans is a base cabinet with a narrow-profile pan drawer. For smaller appliances, consider a rolling cart that disguises itself as a base cabinet when stored away. Pull it out and you have extra counter space, as well as handy access to appliances.

It's no fun dragging a 40-pound bag of pet food out from under the sink every day. To keep the food accessible but out of reach of interested pets, add a pet food bin to your kitchen. It rolls out to help you make quick work of an often-awkward chore.

Some storage solutions are less dramatic, but every bit as useful. Hang a spice rack on the inside of a cabinet door, for instance. Or get the bread box off the counter with a bread-box drawer insert.

EXPERTS' INSIGHT

DON'T OVERDO SPECIALTY CABINETS

Avoid filling your kitchen with too many specialty racks and drawers. Because the sizes of items change and your (or future owners') needs change, it is best to leave at least half of your cabinets plain. You always can add things later. Factory-made cabinets often can be purchased with such racks or special drawers built in. But check out prices before you order; you may be able to save by spending a couple of hours installing systems yourself.

appliance garage

rolling cart

narrow-profile pan drawer

spice rack mounted on inside of door

pet food bin

bread-box drawer

Most kitchens benefit from some open shelving to break the blankness of cabinet doors and to display treasured items. China display shelves and open corner shelves add decorative focal points to your kitchen. With any exposed racks, be sure that they can be cleaned with reasonable ease. Some such racks have removable components. Plates and glasses left exposed may have to be washed every month or so.

A pull-out cutting board saves counter space. The one shown at right hides behind a hinged drawer face; the board is part of a shallow drawer. It can be removed for cleaning and has a groove that collects juices.

Small open shelves underneath wall cabinets are handy for storing recipes. Or they can be used as an organizer for a desk area below them. A range vent faced with a small shelf is more decorative and useful than the usual blank range hood. An undercabinet wine rack looks great and keeps your vintage at hand.

Money $ Saver

PURCHASE A PACKAGE

Most of these variations on standard cabinets can be purchased when you order your cabinet system. Items like this tend to be pricey individually, but you may get a break if they are part of a larger package deal. You'll probably save some money if you order everything at once.

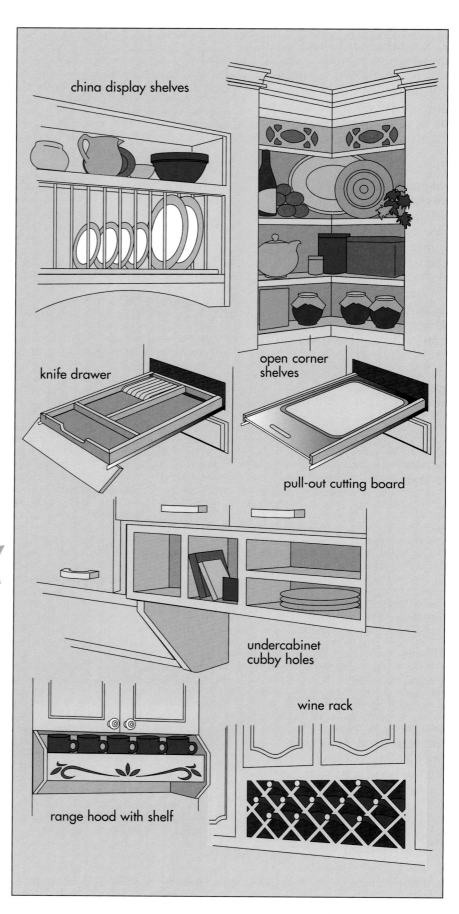

china display shelves

open corner shelves

knife drawer

pull-out cutting board

undercabinet cubby holes

wine rack

range hood with shelf

A small desk in the kitchen is a surprisingly useful idea. Position it away from the main work triangle, especially the range, oven, or cooktop. This handy office area can be used for planning meals, organizing recipes, paying bills, or mapping housekeeping strategies. Let the kids use it for homework, and you will be able to keep an eye on them while you work in the kitchen. The cubbyholes and drawers provide places for those clipped recipes, school schedules, and useful coupons that seem to take over the kitchen.

A stemware rack is another option that is as much an attractive feature as it is a good use of space. Be careful where you position one. Avoid areas where you'll be doing a lot of counter work; you wouldn't want to bump the glasses with your head.

A cozy little shelf under a glass-fronted cabinet is just the right size for teacups or mugs—things you want to display and be able to get at easily.

Most sink bases have false drawer faces because the sink fills the space where a drawer might fit. But there is room for a tilt-out drawer face. This is handy for sponges and brushes that otherwise clutter up the sink area.

A recycling center with two or three bags or bins can be attached to a tilt-out or pull-out door on a base cabinet.

There are other options available from manufacturers: foldaway ironing boards that pull down from the wall or out from a false drawer face; small drawers with clear plastic tops used to store dry foodstuffs, such as rice, flour, or beans; and shelves for a microwave, stereo, or television.

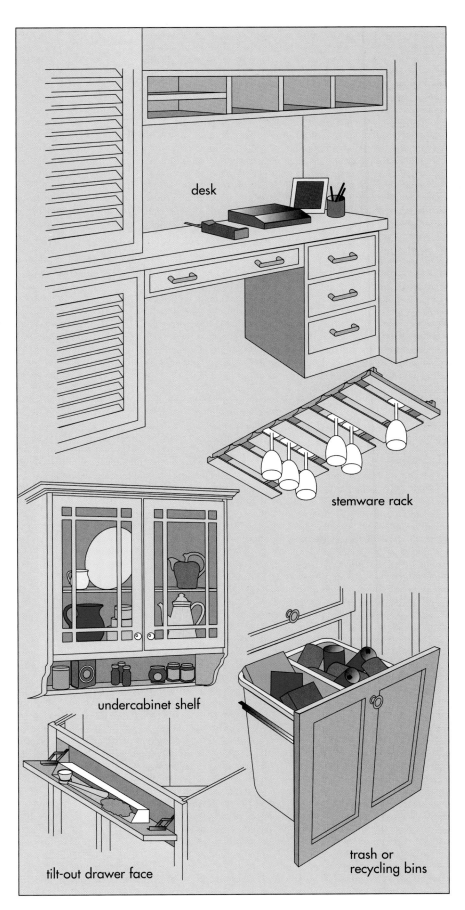

desk

stemware rack

undercabinet shelf

tilt-out drawer face

trash or recycling bins

PLANNING FOR NEW CABINETS

Preparation for installing kitchen cabinets usually is more involved than actually hanging them.

Once you've removed the old cabinets and appliances, install and check plumbing lines, both drain and supply. Run the gas line if needed for a gas cooktop, oven, or range.

Rough in the electrical outlets, switches, and cables for dishwashers. If you will be installing undercabinet lights that are not low-voltage (see page 35), have standard electrical cable sticking out of the walls at points just below the bottom of the wall cabinets. Cut out a vent hole for a range hood (see page 20).

Smooth and prime all wall and ceiling surfaces, especially those that will show after the cabinets are in place. In most cases, it makes sense to install the flooring before installing the cabinets. Piecing around them is difficult and time-consuming. While you may waste material under the cabinets, a smooth finished floor to work on makes the job easier. If you are using expensive flooring, however, you may want to leave the area under the cabinets uncovered. Overlap the footprint of your base cabinets with the flooring. Add pieces of flooring at all four corners to level each cabinet.

Carefully mark the location of each cabinet on the walls. Allow for small spacers at the corners so you will not have to cram things in too tightly. Mark the location of all the wall studs.

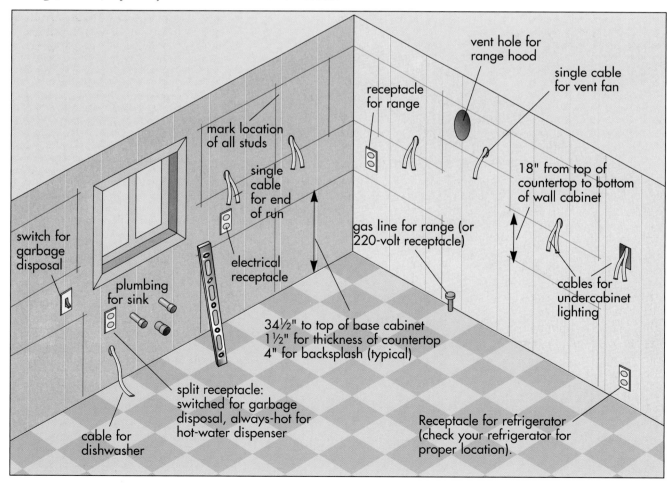

vent hole for range hood

single cable for vent fan

receptacle for range

mark location of all studs

single cable for end of run

18" from top of countertop to bottom of wall cabinet

switch for garbage disposal

electrical receptacle

gas line for range (or 220-volt receptacle)

cables for undercabinet lighting

plumbing for sink

34½" to top of base cabinet
1½" for thickness of countertop
4" for backsplash (typical)

split receptacle: switched for garbage disposal, always-hot for hot-water dispenser

cable for dishwasher

Receptacle for refrigerator (check your refrigerator for proper location).

INSTALLING WALL CABINETS

*T*ake the cabinets out of their boxes and inspect them carefully; you won't be able to return them once you have driven screws into them. If you are installing undercabinet lighting, you may need to drill holes in the back lower lip of the cabinets for the electrical cable to slip through (see page 35).

If your walls are not plumb or square, you may end up with a cabinet that doesn't fit. Check in advance and reposition your layout accordingly.

Always work with a helper, and have a stable stepladder on hand. If any of the cabinets are heavy, remove the doors to reduce the weight and lessen the chance of damaging the cabinets.

YOU'LL NEED

TIME: Several hours for six or seven cabinets.
SKILLS: Leveling, driving screws.
TOOLS: Level, drill with screwdriver bit, clamps.

EXPERTS' INSIGHT

FASTEN WALL CABINETS TO WALL STUDS

If you've carried a stack of 10 or 12 dishes, you know how heavy they are. Cabinets holding dishes or canned goods bear a surprisingly heavy load. Because wall cabinets do not rest on anything, the screws attaching them to the wall carry all the weight. Make sure you drive screws into wall studs. If you are attaching to a masonry wall, use metal masonry shields.

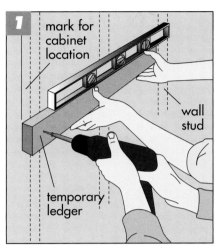

1. Attach a temporary ledger.
Anchor a straight piece of 2×4 lumber to the wall so you can rest the cabinets on it as you work. Level it and attach it with just a few screws or nails, so you won't create a big wall-patching job when you remove it.

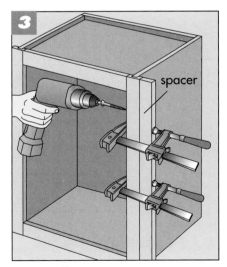

2. Fasten the cabinets.
While a helper holds the cabinet, check for plumb in both directions. Use shims, as shown, if necessary. Once the cabinet is positioned, drive 2½- or 3-inch screws through the cabinet frames and into wall studs. If your cabinet has a lip on top, drive the screws in there so they will not show. Use trim washers for a more finished look on the inside of the cabinet.

3. Install spacers.
Where the last cabinet meets up against a side wall, hold the cabinet in place and measure for a spacer. Cut it and attach as shown, using clamps to hold it firmly while you drill pilot holes and drive screws from the cabinet into the spacer.

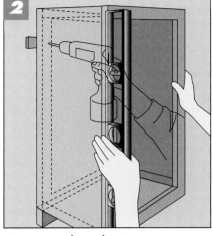

4. Install spacer for inside corner.
If you simply attach two cabinets at an inside corner, usually at least one door will not open fully. Before installing them, attach a spacer to one of the cabinets (see Step 3) and then attach the other cabinet to the spacer. Drill pilot holes and drive in screws.

SETTING BASE CABINETS

Take the time to make sure all the cabinets are level from the beginning. If you give in to the temptation to cheat a little, you will run into frustrating problems, both in installing the other cabinets and in putting on the countertop.

If a baseboard or other piece of molding gets in the way, it is almost always best to take it off the wall and cut it, rather than cutting the cabinet to fit around the trim.

YOU'LL NEED

TIME: Most of a day for an average-size kitchen.
SKILLS: Leveling, driving screws, clamping, cutting.
TOOLS: Drill, level, hammer, chisel, pry bar.

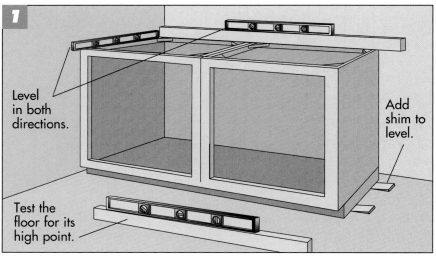

Level in both directions.

Add shim to level.

Test the floor for its high point.

1. Level and plumb the first unit.

Find the highest point on your floor and start there because you can shim up but not down. Set the first cabinet in place and check it for level in both directions. As a further check, make sure the stiles or door faces are plumb. Use shims at the floor to level and solidly support the cabinets. If your wall is out of plumb or wavy, you may need to shim the back of the cabinet as well—make sure when you drive the screws in (see next step) you don't pull the cabinet out of level.

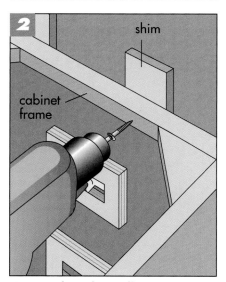

shim

cabinet frame

2. Attach to the walls.

Drive in screws through the back of the cabinet and into the wall studs. When possible, screw through solid framing pieces. After driving in the screws, check to see that the cabinet is still sitting flat on the floor. If not, back out the screws and adjust the shims before driving the screws back in. Check again for level and plumb.

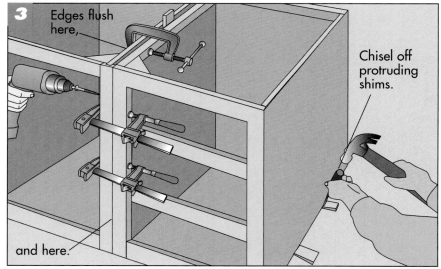

Edges flush here,

and here.

Chisel off protruding shims.

3. Join cabinets together.

After installing the first cabinet, use clamps to hold the next one in alignment as you screw them together. Make sure their surfaces are flush with each other—not just the face frames, but the top edges as well.

Also make sure the screws are the right length, so they will not poke through the stiles. To keep the surface of the stiles smooth, drill pilot and countersink holes, then drive in the screws.

In most cases, you can use a hammer and chisel to nip off shims that stick out. With layers of shim, use a handsaw.

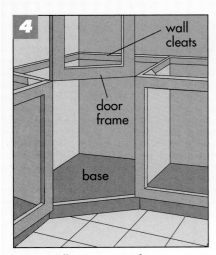

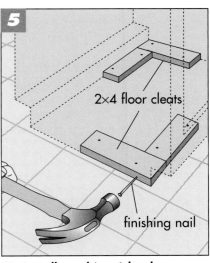

4. Install a corner cabinet...
You may buy a complete corner cabinet with sides or a less-expensive knockdown unit like the one shown above. For this type of corner cabinet, install the base first, then set the two adjoining cabinets in place next to it. Insert the door frame and join it to the adjoining cabinets. Install 1×2 cleats on the walls to support the countertop.

or join two base cabinets.
This method provides you with less usable space, but it may save money. Be sure to install at least one spacer so both doors swing freely. Clamp, drill pilot and countersink holes, and drive in screws.

5. Install a cabinet island.
When there is no wall to attach a cabinet to, as in the case of an island or peninsula, provide strong framing on the floor. Lay the cabinet on its side and measure its inside dimensions. Measure and install 2×4 cleats on the floor carefully so the cabinet slips over the cleats tightly. For exposed areas use finishing nails; otherwise drill pilot holes and use screws.

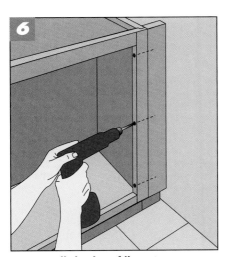

6. Install the last filler piece.
When you come to an inside wall, measure the distance between the cabinet and the wall at both the top and bottom. Rip a filler piece to fit snugly and position it flush with the cabinet face. Drill pilot and countersink holes and drive in screws. Unless the filler piece is more than 4 inches wide, you do not need to attach it to the wall.

7. Install panels.
If your design calls for an exposed edge that is not the side of a cabinet, as is the case when a dishwasher is at the end of a run, purchase an end panel made for the purpose of completing the run. Use clips at the floor, countertop, and wall so the panel can be removed to service the dishwasher.

EXPERTS' INSIGHT

INSTALLATION TIPS
Even durable cabinets made to hold up to decades of normal use can be scratched or dinged easily by carpentry tools. Take special care not to damage cabinets as you work on them. Cover installed cabinets with heavy drop cloths or cardboard from their shipping boxes and keep sharp tools well away from door and drawer faces.

If your floor is out of level or wavy, avoid unsightly gaps at the bottom of your cabinets by installing vinyl cove base. Or remove the kickboard, take out the nails, and reinstall it tight against the floor.

BUILDING AN ISLAND OR PENINSULA

If you purchase custom cabinets, you can design an island or peninsula to suit your needs exactly. If your budget is limited, you can combine standard-sized base cabinets to make your own unit. In both cases, you need to make or have a countertop specialist make a countertop. This simple island, made of two base cabinets, side panels, and a veneered plywood back panel, is simple to construct. The countertop is something most do-it-yourselfers can build. The most difficult part of the project is the installation of electrical cables, gas pipe, plumbing supply and drains, and the vent duct.

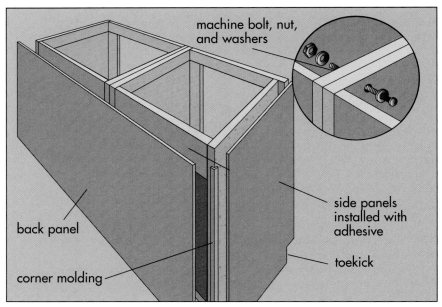

machine bolt, nut, and washers

back panel

corner molding

side panels installed with adhesive

toekick

YOU'LL NEED
TIME: About half a day to build the island.
SKILLS: Basic carpentry, wiring, plumbing.
TOOLS: Screwdriver, drill, adjustable wrench, circular saw, block plane, sandpaper.

Adding a countertop
Plan an island countertop carefully: If it is to be an eating counter, make it wide enough to accommodate seating but not so wide as to hinder traffic flow. Round off exposed corners, to avoid painful encounters.

Countertops usually are made of chipboard, which means they cannot handle much weight if they are not supported from underneath. Make a cantilevered countertop stronger by using plywood attached to a 1×2 frame to thicken the edge. Add bracket supports if you wish to extend the top to make a stool-height informal eating area. Install wood base shoe or vinyl cove base at the bottom. Attach the island to the floor as shown on page 31.

Combining stock cabinets
When using stock base cabinets, you will have access to the shelves from one side only. If you want the countertop to be at a good height for people sitting on stools, trim the cabinets down by cutting off the toekick. To anchor the island to the floor, see page 31.

Join the cabinets together by clamping, drilling pilot holes, and installing bolts. As an alternative, drive general-purpose screws through the frames, being careful not to pierce the other side. Install panels on the sides using construction adhesive. Cover the back with a single panel.

Finish the corners with corner molding. If building a peninsula, vary the design so it butts against your base cabinets.

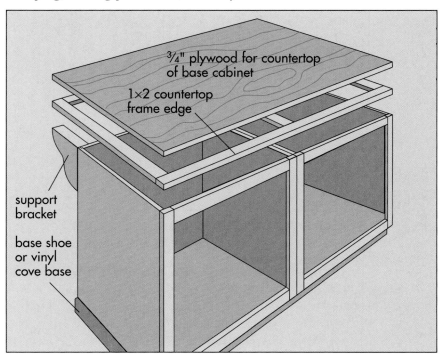

¾" plywood for countertop of base cabinet

1×2 countertop frame edge

support bracket

base shoe or vinyl cove base

Island or peninsula with a sink

A small sink on a island is handy for vegetable preparation, and it's an ideal way to take pressure off the main kitchen sink. If your plans include a sink, your biggest problem likely will be getting the drain to the sink. If you have a basement with exposed joists below, the job will be fairly easy. If not, you will have to open up the ceiling below or the kitchen floor. Drain pipes must flow downhill.

More important, drains must be properly vented (see page 87). If you are moving more than 5 feet away from a vented waste stack, you may have to supply a new vent (check your local codes), a job that may require the help of a professional plumber.

Water supply lines are less of a problem, particularly if you have a basement or crawlspace under the kitchen. See pages 48–49 for how to install a sink, page 50 for faucet installation instructions, page 67 for installing a trap, and page 91 for how to install stop valves.

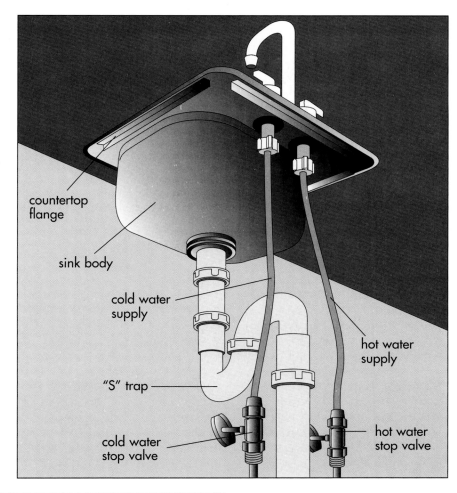

countertop flange

sink body

cold water supply

"S" trap

cold water stop valve

hot water supply

hot water stop valve

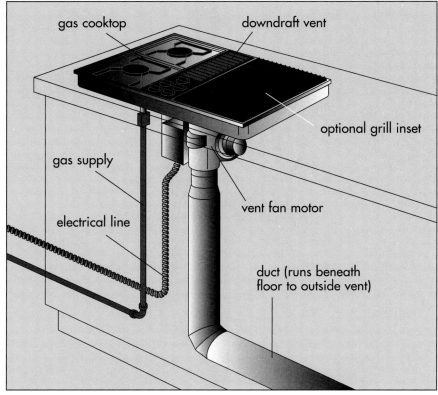

gas cooktop

downdraft vent

gas supply

electrical line

optional grill inset

vent fan motor

duct (runs beneath floor to outside vent)

Downdraft range

An island cooktop should be vented. If your island or peninsula has overhead cabinets, you can install a vent hood. But usually a downdraft range is the best choice for an island or peninsula. These appliances have a vent fan already installed as part of the units. You will need to run not only a gas line, but also an electrical line for the fan. (For an electric range, hire an electrician to run a 220-volt line to the unit.)

The ductwork is simple to understand but often difficult to install. The easiest way is to run it through the basement or crawlspace below the kitchen. If that is not possible, you may have to cut large holes in floor joists, but only if the structural integrity can be maintained. The vent exits the house in the same way as a range hood vent.

ADDING UNDERCABINET HALOGEN LIGHTING

A kitchen is cheerier and more user-friendly when its countertops are well illuminated by undercabinet fixtures. As with any working area, adequate lighting makes tasks easier.

If your wall cabinets are correctly placed (54 inches above the floor, 18 inches above the countertop) the lights will be below eye level.

A halogen system like the one shown usually comes as a kit, with built-in limitations: The number of lights and the length of the wires may be predetermined. Plan the job before you purchase the lights.

YOU'LL NEED

TIME: About 1 day to install a switch and 10 lights.
SKILLS: Stripping and connecting wires, simple carpentry.
TOOLS: Screwdriver, drill, lineman's pliers, keyhole saw.

MEASUREMENTS

HOW MUCH LIGHTING DO YOU NEED?

The low-voltage halogen lighting shown here is the simplest solution, especially if the cabinets are installed already. But if you are in the process of installing cabinets or if you do not like halogen lights, install thin (1"–1½" thick) fluorescent units under the cabinets (see page 35). If you're installing undercabinet fluorescent lighting, plan on one 20-watt unit per 3 running feet of countertop. For halogens, use one 12-watt unit per 3 feet. For incandescent lights you should use one 75-watt unit per every 3 feet of countertop.

1. Install lights, transformer.
Determine a location for each light fixture: It should not shine in your eyes as you work at the countertop, and it should not be near combustible material—halogen lamps get hot.

Remove the trim ring and lens from each light fixture and attach them with screws to the underside of the cabinets. Be sure the screws are the right length so they do not

poke up into your cabinet.

Drill small holes to allow the wires to pass into the cabinet. Plug the ends of the wires into the power block, which is mounted inside the cabinet. Run another wire to the transformer. Because the wires cannot be cut, you will have to hide coils of wire inside the cabinet. Finally, drill a hole and run a wire from a receptacle to the transformer.

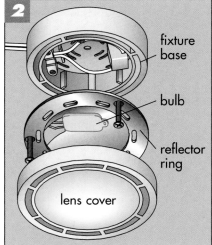

2. Assemble the lights.
Plug the halogen bulb into the socket. Install the lens cover. Your kit should come with a CAUTION label, warning that the bulbs are hot. Stick it in a place where guests in your kitchen can see it.

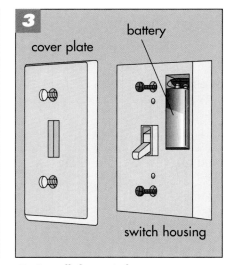

3. Install the switch.
The switch operates by battery power, so it can be installed anywhere and requires no wiring. Attach the switch housing by screwing it into the wall. Use plastic anchors if you cannot find a stud to attach it to. Screw the cover plate to the housing.

INSTALLING FLUORESCENT LIGHTING

Like halogens, fluorescent lights are more energy-efficient than incandescent bulbs. Because they produce little heat and are available in a variety of sizes, you can place them wherever you choose. The most common method of installation is to run standard electrical cable behind the walls (see pages 94–97). If the wires run behind the cabinets, you will not have to patch walls. No wires will be exposed if you tuck the fixture against the wall. Or use raceway wiring attached to the underside of the cabinets.

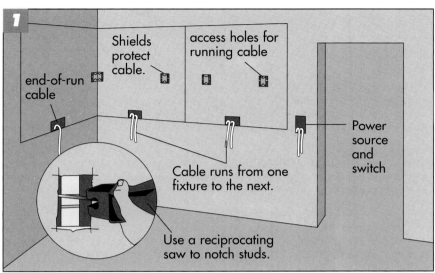

1 Shields protect cable.
end-of-run cable
access holes for running cable
Power source and switch
Cable runs from one fixture to the next.
Use a reciprocating saw to notch studs.

YOU'LL NEED

TIME: With the cabinets removed, a day for an average-size kitchen.
SKILLS: Cutting holes in walls, fishing electrical cable through walls, making connections.
TOOLS: Knife, hammer, chisel, wire strippers, lineman's pliers.

1. Run the cable.
Inspect your cabinets and determine exactly where the cables should emerge from the walls. If the cabinets have a lip in the rear, drill holes in it for the cables to run through. (If your cabinets don't have a lip, you'll have to position the light fixtures against the wall so no cable will be exposed to view.) As often as possible, make holes in places where the cabinets will cover the openings. If a hole will be exposed, cut carefully so patching will be minimal. Run power to the switch, then to the lights. Until the end of a run, two cables must enter each fixture. Install cabinets after running the cables.

EXPERTS' INSIGHT

COVE LIGHTING

■ If your wall cabinets do not butt up against a soffit, consider adding a dramatic lighting effect by placing fluorescent fixtures on top of the cabinets. A piece of cove molding hides the bulbs from view. The light will be directed upward for a halo effect around your kitchen.

■ Installing cove lighting is easy because there is little wiring to hide. Simply run exposed cables and place the fixtures on top of the cabinets toward the rear. **Note:** Be sure to shut off the power.

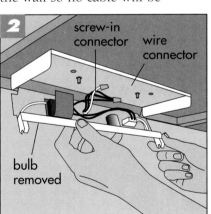

2 screw-in connector wire connector
bulb removed

2. Make the connections.
Open the fixture, punch out the knockout, and install the screw-in connectors. (If your unit is only 1 inch thick, you will need a special reducing connector.) Fasten the fixture base to the cabinet. Strip the wires and make connections. Seal the connections with wire connectors (see page 95). Make sure there are no exposed areas of uninsulated wire.

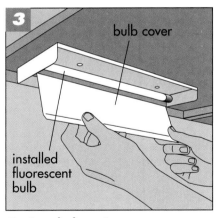

3 bulb cover
installed fluorescent bulb

3. Attach the units.
Carefully close the fixture housing without cramming or pinching wires and fasten it to the fixture base. Install the fluorescent bulb and plastic bulb cover. For larger fluorescent units, consider installing a strip of wood along the lower front edge of the cabinet to ensure that the light is shielded fully from view.

CHOOSING COUNTERTOPS

Next to cabinets, countertops do the most to set the style of your kitchen. In addition, they are working surfaces that need to be made of a material you are comfortable with. A number of options are available, all of which do the job well. They range from inexpensive post-form laminates you can buy at a home center (only a few colors will be available) to high-priced granite and solid-surface materials.

Wood, such as maple butcher block, is also an option. But such countertops require careful maintenance: Keep them well waxed or give them regular applications of mineral oil. Otherwise, the countertop will discolor and possibly start coming apart at the seams.

Solid-surface
These are durable and can accommodate a seamless sink. They come in a variety of colors and patterns, many of which rival stone. Their cost rivals stone as well; consider this material among the most expensive countertop options. This is not a do-it-yourself material; solid-surface countertops must be fabricated and installed by specialists.

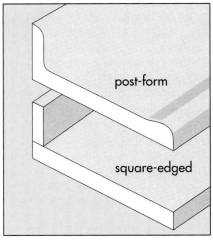

Laminate
Color-core laminates withstand scratches better than laminates on which the color is applied only on the surface. You can buy a ready-made post-form, with either a rolled front edge and a built-in backsplash or a square-edged top. With patience, you can laminate a square-edge top yourself, but the cost of materials may be nearly as much as a factory-made top.

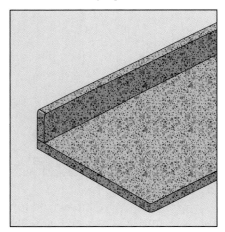

Granite
This beautiful natural product provides decades of use if installed properly. You must hire a contractor to measure and install it for you; they know how to handle this heavy material and have equipment for buffing all the surfaces to a shine. Marble is not recommended as countertop material because it stains easily.

Tile
There are many colors and sizes of tile from which to choose. Be sure the edging and backsplash pieces come in the colors you want. Avoid wall tiles. They are not made to take impact and chip easily. Some people find the grout joints hard to clean; others dislike an uneven surface. But well-installed tile is durable and stylish.

INSTALLING A LAMINATE COUNTERTOP

You can make your own laminate countertop. Unless you are skilled do-it-yourselfer, however, it may not be worth the time and effort. If your countertop configuration is fairly typical, you can save money by purchasing post-form countertops from your home center. Made with precut corners, these countertops can be trimmed to fit most base cabinets.

But if you don't like the colors available at your home center or if you have an unusual situation, such as a wide counter for an island or a narrow counter for a tight spot, you will need to have a countertop made for you. You may have a wider selection of color and pattern if you choose a square-edge top rather than a post-form (see page 36).

YOU'LL NEED

TIME: Half a day to install several tops carefully.
SKILLS: General carpentry, working carefully to avoid damaging the tops as you work.
TOOLS: Level, carpenter's square, drill, circular saw, compass, belt sander, laundry iron.

CAUTION!
BE SURE THE TOP HUGS YOUR WALLS

If you have a wavy wall or if your walls are more than 3/8 inch out of square, a ready-made top may not fit snugly against your walls. Take measures to straighten out your walls or hire a professional countertop maker to come in and take precise measurements so a custom countertop can be made to fit your space.

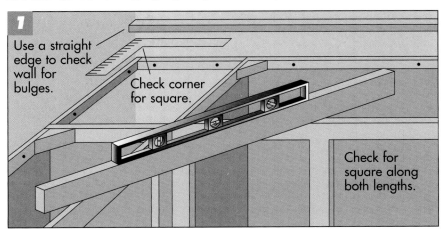

Use a straight edge to check wall for bulges.

Check corner for square.

Check for square along both lengths.

1. Check walls, cabinets for level and square.
Make sure cabinets are level all around so the top will be able to sit flat on them. If necessary, install cleats on walls, as shown, or end panels (see page 31) to support the top firmly. Check walls to ensure they are square with each other and free of major bulges by laying a straightedge down the full length of each. Most post-forms have a "scribe," a lip of laminate that can be trimmed (see below) to compensate for variations of up to 3/8 inch. A square-edged top with a separate backsplash will let you compensate for up to 3/4 inch.

temporary guide

2. Cut a top to length.
If you purchase a factory-made top that you must cut yourself, do this with great care. Use a fine-cutting blade and cut it with the face side down to avoid nicks. Check that the blade on your circular saw is square to the base and use a clamp-on guide to make sure your cut is straight. Be sure to support the waste side so it does not fall off before you finish the cut—an easy way to chip laminate.

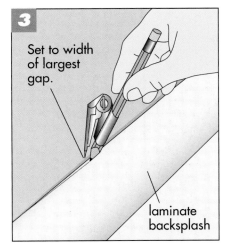

Set to width of largest gap.

laminate backsplash

3. Scribe a backsplash line.
The countertop might not fit tight against the wall, either because the walls are out of square or the wall is wavy. If such is the case, push the countertop against the wall, making sure it is aligned correctly with the base cabinets. Use a compass to scribe a line as wide as the largest gap between the countertop and the wall.

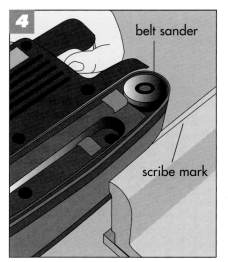

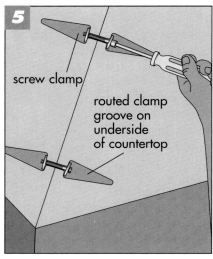

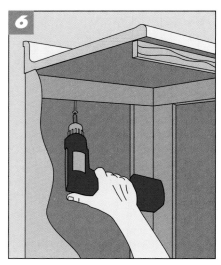

4. Belt-sand to the scribe mark.

Don't attempt to cut to the scribe mark with a sabersaw or circular saw—you'll almost certainly end up chipping the countertop. Use a belt sander with a fairly coarse 36-grit sanding belt. Pressing lightly, slowly sand away material up to the scribed mark.

5. Make a splice.

If you need to splice pieces at a corner or in the middle of a run, have a professional make the cuts and rout the grooves for the clamps. Apply waterproof glue to the edges of the pieces, line up the pieces, and start to tighten the clamps. Check the countertop as you work to make sure it doesn't slide out of alignment.

6. Attach the top to the cabinets.

Screws should extend as far into the countertop as possible without poking through it. Drill pilot holes every 2 to 3 feet along the front and rear of the top and drive in screws upward to hold the counter firmly. Screw into structurally sound sections of the cabinet framing. Make sure the countertop does not move as you work.

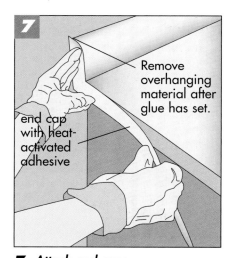

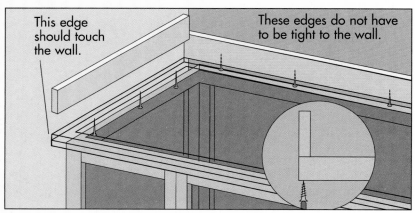

7. Attach end caps.

Buy a precut end cap to cover the end of a post form. If it has heat-activated glue, hold it in place so it overhangs the countertop edge. (You'll remove the excess later.) Slowly run a hot laundry iron along the end cap, being careful not to burn the laminate, until the glue adheres. File, sand, or rout away the excess material.

Install a square-edged countertop.

If you buy a square-edged countertop and your walls are not square, this type of edging covers up the gap. Set the top so it overhangs the cabinets evenly. Cut the backsplash pieces to fit and set them in place. Mark their position on the countertop, then pull the top away from the wall. Run a bead of bathtub caulk along the bottom of the edging, set the edging in place, and fasten it with screws from underneath. Attach the top from underneath as shown in Step 6. If your wall bows, fasten the top in place, then glue the edging pieces to the wall with construction adhesive. Brace them with pieces of 1× or heavy objects so the edging conforms to the wall.

SETTING A TILE COUNTERTOP

Choose tiles made for use on countertops. That usually means the tiles are ½ inch thick. They should be glazed, or they will stain easily. Use a light-colored grout or a grout that comes close to the color of the tile, rather than a dark, starkly contrasting color that will emphasize any imperfections or variations.

To be sure the tile color and finish is consistent, work with a tile dealer who can supply all the types of tile you'll need. These include field tiles (the square tiles that cover the bulk of the counter), decorative or bullnose tiles for the front edge, and bullnose pieces for the backsplash. Each tile that has an exposed edge must have a rounded edge, called a bullnose or cap, on that edge. Don't use a field tile and then give it a finished edge with grout; it looks bad and wears poorly.

Choose the mastic recommended by the tile dealer. Usually, this is a thinset mortar. All-purpose tile adhesive will not hold up on countertops.

Work slowly and systematically. Although setting a tile countertop looks complicated, it is an ideal weekend project well within the range of most do-it-yourselfers.

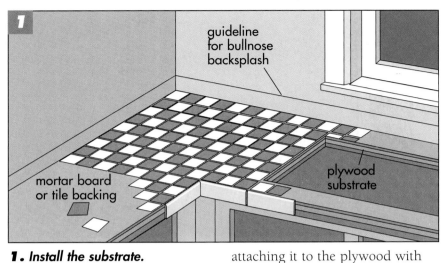

guideline for bullnose backsplash

mortar board or tile backing

plywood substrate

1. Install the substrate.
Tiles must be set on a firm, level, and perfectly flat surface. Be sure the total thickness of the substrate, including the mastic, will be covered by the edging you choose (see page 40). Begin by securely attaching ⅝- or ¾-inch plywood to the top of the cabinets. Check the substrate for level and square. Cover the substrate with a layer of mortar board or tile backing,

attaching it to the plywood with screws placed in a grid pattern, no more than 4 inches apart.

If you will be using backsplash edging tile with a large radius, provide backing for it by fastening a strip of mortar board to the wall. Though hard to find, you may be able to buy a metal screed for the front edge. It offers a straight line for setting tile and a surface to which the mastic can adhere.

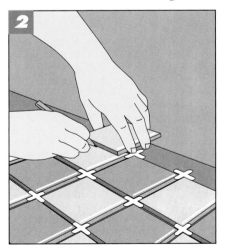

2. Lay out a dry run.
Set the tiles in place, positioning them exactly as you want the finished surface to look. Use plastic spacers, and check that all your lines are straight. To mark tiles for cutting, hold them in place rather than measuring. Always remember to allow for the thickness of the grout joint.

YOU'LL NEED
TIME: A full day to install about 12 feet of countertop tile; then 2 to 3 hours the following day to grout the tile.
SKILLS: Cutting and fastening plywood, measuring and cutting tiles, grouting.
TOOLS: Knife, drill, notched trowel, tile cutter, nibbling tool, bedding block, grout float, sponge.

EXPERTS' INSIGHT

OTHER METHODS OF SETTING TILE COUNTERTOPS
■ Professionals often set tiles in a bed of mortar about 1 inch thick. This is slightly more durable than the method shown here, but it takes skill to lay down a level mortar bed.
■ Don't simply apply mastic to a plywood surface and set tiles as you would wall tile. Some moisture always seeps through the grout joints of tile counter-tops. Ordinary mastics, weakened by the moisture, won't protect the substrate and the plywood will get damaged.

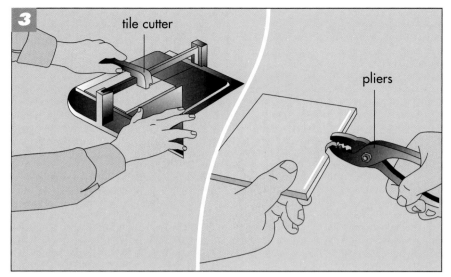

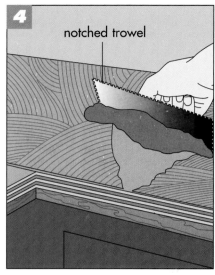

3. Cut the tiles.

For straight cuts, use a tile cutter. It uses a glass-cutting wheel to score the tile and a lever to break off a straight cut. Your tile supplier may provide a cutter free of charge. If not, tile cutters can be rented. But if your project will take several weekends it may be less expensive to buy one.

To cut a tile, position it on the cutter and bear down firmly as you score a single line. Then snap the cut by pushing down on the handle. The best tile cutters have adjustable guides, enabling you to quickly cut a series of tiles all the same size.

If you have a lot of straight cuts to do, rent a tile-cutting wet saw (see page 42). For occasional cutouts or curves, use pliers or a nibbling tool to bite away the tile bit by bit.

4. Apply the mastic.

Mix the thinset mortar according to directions. If the powder does not contain latex additive, mix with latex rather than water. Allow the mixture to "slake" for 10 minutes, then mix again. Pick up a section of the dry-laid tiles and apply the mortar to the surface with the proper-size notched trowel. Set each section before moving on to the next section.

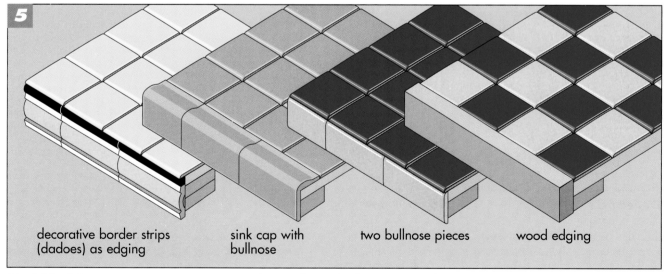

decorative border strips (dadoes) as edging   sink cap with bullnose   two bullnose pieces   wood edging

5. Add edging.

Bring color and interest to your countertop by edging it with a combination of decorative border strips (dadoes) overlapped by bullnose tiles.

A sink cap provides a slight lip that keeps water from dripping down the edge of the counter. It may have a lower bullnose edge of its own, or you may have to add a row of bullnose tiles under it.

Another alternative is two bullnose edging pieces (also called caps), one on the counter surface, one on the edging. Install the edge pieces and the surface tiles at the same time to keep them aligned.

Wood edging goes on after tiles are set. Make sure it is protected with a durable finish. Set the top edge of the wood slightly below the tile surface so you can wipe the counter easily. Join the edging to the plywood with trim screws, or use a biscuit joiner so no screw holes have to be puttied.

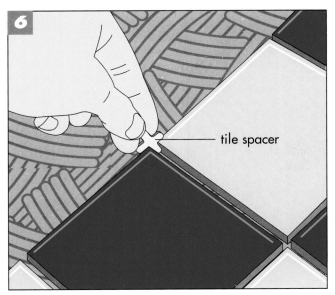

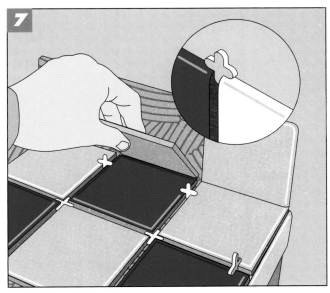

6. Lay the tiles.

As you set the tiles in place, try to put them right where you want them. Avoid sliding them too much. Use plastic spacers to keep the joints even. As you work, make sure the tiles evenly overlap, or line up with, the edge pieces.

7. Tile a backsplash.

If you will be using backsplash tiles of the same width as the field tiles, line them up so the grout joints match. These tiles will not receive the same wear as the top tiles, so you can glue them directly to the wall without a plywood substrate.

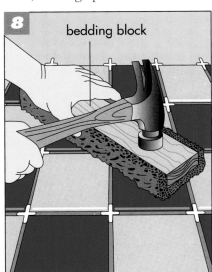

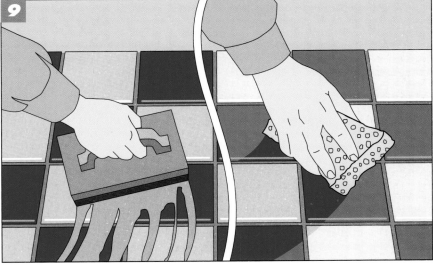

8. Bed the tiles.

After you've finished an area, bed the tiles to make sure they set down into the mastic and form a smooth, even surface. Use a bedding block made of a scrap of wood wrapped with a piece of carpet. Tap gently with a hammer or rubber mallet.

9. Grout, wipe, and buff.

Allow the tiles to set at least 24 hours. Mix your grout according to directions. If you are using colored grout, mix the dry ingredients together thoroughly. Use latex grout additive rather than water to keep the grout from cracking. Mix, allow to slake for 10 minutes, then mix again.

Apply with a grout float in two steps. First, push the grout into the joints by holding the float fairly flat. Move the float in at least two directions so all the cracks are filled in completely. Second, tip the float up at a fairly steep angle and wipe away the excess.

Use a damp sponge to wipe away more excess grout, checking each grout line to ensure it is filled evenly. Rinse the sponge often; it will take two or three spongings to remove most of the residue on top of the tiles. After the grout is dry, remove the final film from the tile surface by rubbing it with a dry cloth. The tiles will shine.

SETTING GRANITE TILE

Here's how to get a long-lasting and stylish granite surface at a fraction of the cost of a granite slab countertop. You'll have small joint lines, but they won't be as noticeable as those of a ceramic tile surface. To keep the look as seamless as possible, use narrow grouted joints. Or you can eliminate the grout altogether by butting the pieces tightly against each other. The silicone caulk used as adhesive has the added benefit of protecting the plywood substrate. Make sure the substrate is level, square, and smooth.

YOU'LL NEED

TIME: About 1 day for a 12-foot-long countertop.
SKILL: Cutting tiles, careful alignment of tiles.
TOOLS: Wet saw, caulking gun.

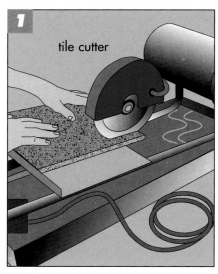

1. Cut tiles, do a dry run.
To cut granite, you must use a wet saw, which you can rent. Because silicone caulk sets quickly, do a complete dry run by cutting and placing every tile before you start gluing. Make sure every piece fits exactly where you want it.

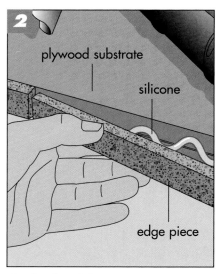

2. Apply edging.
Cut narrow strips of granite of an equal depth to give the edge a uniform appearance. This requires careful cutting. Plan on having to discard miscut pieces. The pieces should fit under the overhanging surface pieces and hang about ¼ inch below the substrate edge.

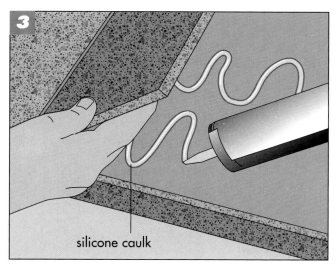

3. Set tiles with silicone.
Pick up two or three tiles, leaving the others unmoved. Using a caulking gun, apply squiggles of clear silicone caulk to the plywood in a close, regular pattern. Immediately set the tile in place and move quickly to the next tile. Press down so the surface is uniform. Have the front edges of the top tiles buffed. (Your tile dealer can recommend a professional who does this.) Or brush on several coats of clear lacquer. Finish with a granite sealer.

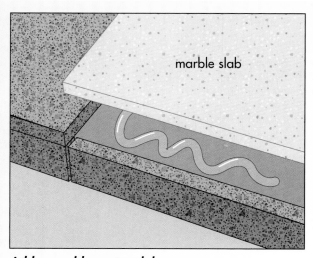

Add a marble pastry slab.
A permanently installed piece of marble makes a great pastry slab. Shop for marble of the same thickness as the granite tile. If the marble is more than ⅛ inch thicker than the granite, you'll have to add a layer of plywood beneath the area to be covered with granite so the final surface will be even. Install the marble with silicone caulk or use a white thinset mortar.

ADDING A STAINLESS-STEEL BACKSPLASH

Here's an unusual touch for a household kitchen—a stainless-steel backsplash. It looks stylish and provides a commercial-grade, easy-to-maintain surface between your countertop and the wall cabinets.

The first step is to find a source of the material. If your home center or hardware store can't help you, check in the Yellow Pages under stainless steel or sheet metal. Find a shop that can provide pieces of stainless steel to the exact length you want. Often, stainless steel has to be ordered from a specialty supplier, so schedule accordingly.

Check your measurements or provide a template to be sure you get the correct sizes of pieces. Although it is extremely hard, stainless steel can be damaged during installation. As you work, support the material so it doesn't crimp or get scratched because stainless steel is expensive.

YOU'LL NEED
TIME: A day for several pieces with a few outlet cutouts.
SKILLS: Measuring, checking for square, drilling, cutting metal.
TOOLS: Square, tape measure, drill, sabersaw

TOOLS TO USE

IF YOU MUST CUT STAINLESS STEEL
You can make rough cuts around outlets because the edges will be covered up. But it's hard to make a straight, smooth cut in this amazingly hard material. Use a drill to start the hole, then cut the opening with a sabersaw with a metal-cutting blade designed for cutting stainless steel.

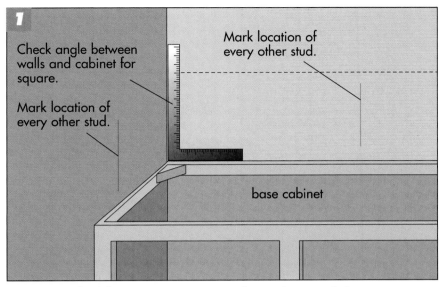

1. Lay out the job.
If possible, do this job before installing the countertop or backsplash and the wall cabinets. Check the walls for square and measure the lengths you need. Corners are the critical areas; any variation along the length of the piece will be covered by the wall cabinet above and the countertop or backsplash below. If your walls are plumb, you may be able to get away without the corner trim pieces shown in Step 3. If the walls are out of plumb, you may be able to compensate by cutting a slot in the corner and sliding a bit of one piece of steel into it.

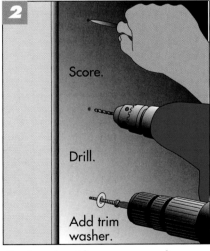

2. Attach with screws, washers.
Set the metal in place and make sure the pieces line up. Drill holes and drive stainless-steel screws, fitted with trim washers, into studs. Because the material is rigid and will be anchored by the cabinets as well, two screws driven in every other stud are adequate.

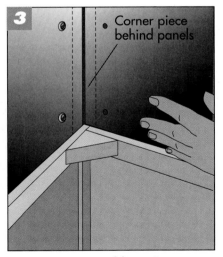

3. Use corner molding pieces.
If you have trouble getting the corners to match up, use a corner mold, attaching it to the wall with clear silicone sealant and butting each panel against it. If one wall is wavy, you can, with patience, scribe and curve-cut one of the pieces using a belt sander.

INSTALLING A DISHWASHER

Replacing a dishwasher is fairly simple. Most units fit neatly into a 24-inch-wide undercounter cavity. All are prewired and ready for simple supply, drainage, and electrical hookups. Installing a new unit, however, is a much bigger job. You must make room for it and bring in electrical, supply, and drain lines. To avoid straining the discharge pump, position the dishwasher as near to the sink as possible.

YOU'LL NEED

TIME: About 2 hours to replace a dishwasher; a full day or more to put in a new one.
SKILLS: Simple plumbing and electrical skills for replacing; carpentry and basic plumbing and electrical skills for a new installation.
TOOLS: Drill, electrical tools, carpentry tools, screwdriver, tongue-and-groove pliers.

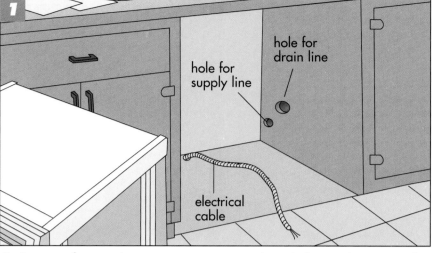

1. Prepare the opening.
Note: *Shut off the water and the electrical power.* To replace an existing dishwasher, remove its lower panel and disconnect the supply line, the drain hose, and the electrical line. Remove any screws attaching it to the countertop and carefully pull the unit out.

For a new installation, remove a 24-inch-wide base cabinet or tailor a space in which you can fit the dishwasher. Bore holes large enough for the supply and drain lines near the lower back of the side panel of the adjoining sink cabinet. A dishwasher needs its own 15- or 20-amp circuit. Run a circuit from the service panel. (You may want to hire a licensed electrician to do this.)

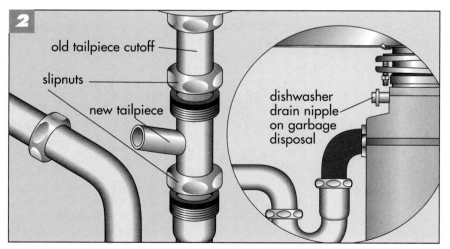

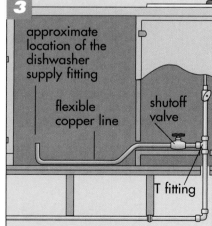

2. Provide a drain fitting.
Your dishwasher can drain either into the sink drain or into a garbage disposal if you have one.

For sink drainage, install a dishwasher tailpiece. Loosen the slipnuts and remove the tailpiece, insert the dishwasher tailpiece into the trap, and cut the old tailpiece to fit above it. Connect all the pieces and tighten the slip nuts.

To drain a dishwasher into a garbage disposal, use a screwdriver and hammer to remove the metal knockout inside the dishwasher drain nipple located near the top of the disposal. The knockout, when freed, may fall into the grinding chamber of the disposal, so be sure to take it out.

3. Run the supply line.
Cut into a convenient hot water supply line, usually the one under the sink. Install a standard T fitting, a nipple, and a shutoff valve. Run flexible copper tubing into the cavity, leaving enough line to reach the dishwasher supply fitting. (See pages 86–91 for basic plumbing instructions.)

4. Attach the drain line.

Thread the drain line through the hole in the cabinet and slip it onto the dishwasher tailpiece or drain nipple—you may have to push hard. Secure it with a hose clamp. To ensure proper operation of the appliance, the drain line must make a loop, as shown at top right, so at some point it is raised near the height of the countertop. Because it vibrates during use, support the drain line securely by wrapping a couple lengths of insulated wire around it and fastening them to screws driven into the underside of the countertop. Take care that the screws do not poke through the countertop.

Some local codes require an air gap (see inset) at the top of the loop. You can place this in a knockout hole in the sink or drill a hole for it in the countertop. Run one line from the drain nipple to the air gap, another from the air gap to the dishwasher drain outlet.

5. Make the hookups.

Position the ends of the three lines about where they will be connected to the dishwasher. Remove the bottom front cover plate from the dishwasher and slide the unit carefully into place, making sure no lines are damaged. Make sure the dishwasher is all the way in position.

Make the connections as shown in the detail drawings. Tighten the compression nut and drain line hose clamp firmly and make secure electrical connections.

Level the dishwasher by turning the leveling screws on the legs. Anchor it to the underside of the countertop with short screws. Turn on the water and the electrical power. Before reattaching the access panel, run the washer through a complete cycle, watching carefully for leaks.

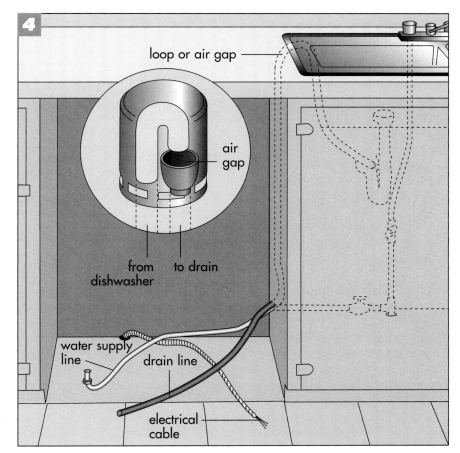

loop or air gap

air gap

from dishwasher

to drain

water supply line

drain line

electrical cable

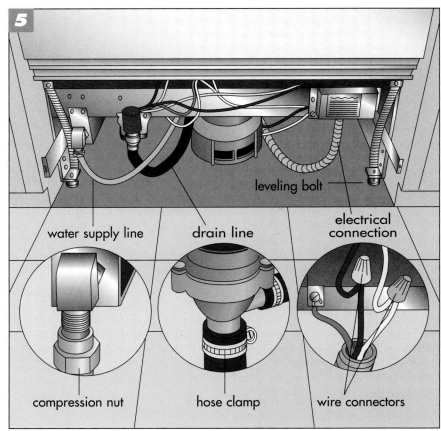

leveling bolt

water supply line

drain line

electrical connection

compression nut

hose clamp

wire connectors

INSTALLING A GARBAGE DISPOSAL

A garbage disposal is a handy kitchen upgrade that is fairly simple to install. Begin by installing a switched electrical receptacle, or buy a self-switching disposal, which you can plug into a standard, always-live receptacle.

If you're installing a new sink, attach the disposal to the sink before you set the sink in place. Otherwise, use plenty of towels to make the undersink work space as comfortable as possible.

YOU'LL NEED

TIME: 2 to 3 hours, not including adding a receptacle and switch.
SKILLS: Basic electrical and plumbing connections.
TOOLS: Hammer, spud wrench, screwdriver, tongue-and-groove pliers, putty knife, wire stripper.

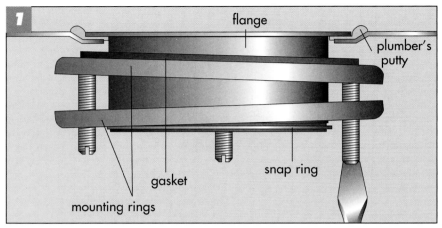

1. Install the mounting assembly.
Disconnect the sink trap and remove the basket strainer. Clean away all old putty. Take apart the mounting assembly by removing the snap ring, mounting rings, and gasket from the flange. Lay a rope of plumber's putty around the sink opening. Have a helper hold the flange in place as you work from underneath. Slip the gasket, mounting rings, and snap ring up onto the flange. The snap ring keeps the mounting assembly in place temporarily. Tighten the mounting assembly against the sink by tightening each screw clockwise a little at a time to assure a tight seal. Using a putty knife, shave away excess putty.

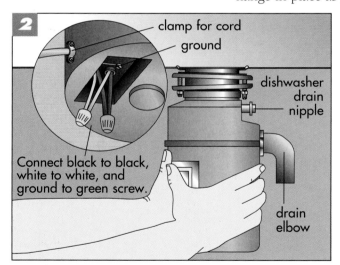

2. Connect electric cord and mount disposal.
Remove the electrical cover plate on the disposal. Strip insulation from the wires of an approved appliance cord, slip it into the opening, and clamp it. Make the electrical connections, gently push the wires into the cavity, and reinstall the cover plate. Secure the drain elbow to the disposal. If you'll drain a dishwasher through the unit, remove the knockout inside the nipple. Position the disposal and rotate it until it engages and tightens. Once the connection is made, rotate the disposal to the best position for attaching the drain lines.

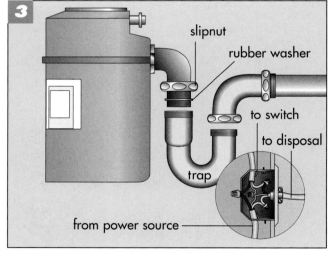

3. Connect to drain line and electrical box.
Fit a slip nut and rubber washer onto the drain elbow, then fasten the trap to the elbow and the drainpipe. You may need to cut the elbow to make the connection. (For double sinks, connect the elbow to the second bowl drain.) Connect the dishwasher drain hose to the drain nipple of the disposal and fasten it with a hose clamp. If you're using a regular electrical receptacle, simply plug in the electrical cord. For a hard-wired installation, shut off the power and connect the wires as shown. Restore power and test for leaks and excessive vibration.

ADDING A HOT WATER DISPENSER

A hot water dispenser is handy for quickly preparing tea, coffee, or instant soup and getting a jump on heating frozen vegetables. The unit itself is easy to install; the most difficult part of this project may be installing an unswitched (always-live) receptacle under your sink. The unit has a thermostat that automatically turns on and off to maintain a temperature of 200°F.

YOU'LL NEED

TIME: About 3 hours, not including installation of an electrical receptacle.
SKILLS: Drilling a clean hole, carefully handling flexible line, basic electrical skills.
TOOLS: Drill, holesaw or metal-boring holesaw, screwdriver, tongue-and-groove pliers, wire strippers.

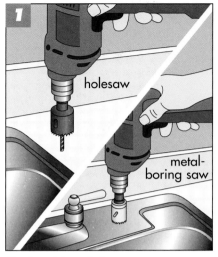

1. Provide a hole.
If your sink has a knockout hole of the correct size, simply punch it out from below. Otherwise, locate a hole so the dispenser's spout hangs over the sink. Drill through the countertop with a holesaw. If you have a stainless-steel sink, you can buy a metal-boring holesaw. Drill slowly.

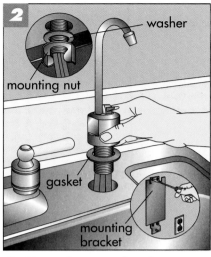

2. Mount faucet and tank.
Insert the assembly with its gasket. With a helper holding it, crawl underneath and tightly attach the washer and mounting nut. Use screws to fasten the tank mounting bracket to the wall. Make sure it is plumb and 12 to 14 inches below the underside of the countertop. Mount the tank on the bracket.

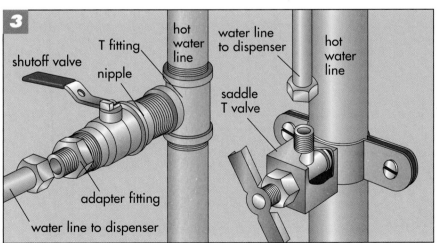

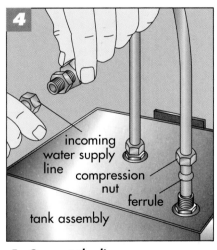

3. Install a water supply valve.
Note: *Shut off the water and drain the line.* To supply the unit with water, tap into the hot water line serving the sink. Cut into the line and install a standard T fitting (see page 91). Add a nipple and a shutoff valve. You'll need an adapter fitting to make the transition to a flexible copper water line that matches the dispenser's supply line.

   If your local building codes permit it, an easier way is to use a saddle T valve. Don't use the puncture-type saddle T, however. Although it is easier to install, it clogs easily. Instead, drill a small hole in the supply line, then secure the saddle valve clamp to the line, as shown above.

4. Connect the lines.
Secure the two longer tubes to the tank assembly and the shorter one to the water supply tube with compression fittings (see page 90). The longer tubes will be coded to make it clear where each goes. Restore water pressure and check for leaks. Always let the tank fill before plugging in or turning on the unit.

INSTALLING A NEW SINK

Whether chipped, stained, or too shallow to be useful, every sink eventually may need replacement. The good news is sink replacement is one of the quickest and most dramatic changes you can make in your kitchen. Because most sinks are rimmed, meaning they have a lip that sits on top of the countertop, installing them is a simple matter of clamping or adhering them to the countertop, then installing the plumbing connections.

YOU'LL NEED

TIME: Half a day to remove an old sink and install a new one, with minor plumbing changes.
SKILLS: Basic plumbing skills.
TOOLS: Sabersaw, straightedge, tongue-and-groove pliers, spud wrench screwdriver, putty knife.

EXPERTS' INSIGHT

TYPES OF SINKS

■ Stainless-steel sinks are inexpensive and long-lasting. The more nickel and chrome in the steel, the more shiny and pricey the sink will be. If you have a garbage disposal, buy an 18-gauge sink to cut down on vibration. Buy units with sound-deadening undercoating.
■ Cast-iron sinks with enamel or porcelain finishes cost more and look classier. They make less noise and clean up easier. Once chipped, however, they are almost impossible to repair.
■ Sinks made of plastic or composite material are increasingly popular. The better ones remain shiny after many scrubbings; the cheaper ones dull.

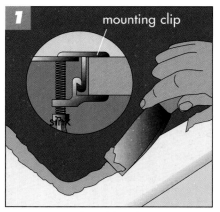

1. Remove the old sink.
Note: *Turn off the water and drain the line.* Disconnect the water supply lines and the trap joining the sink to the drainpipe. Remove mounting clips from underneath by unscrewing them and pushing them to the side. Be sure you get them all. Pry the sink up carefully without scratching the countertop. Clean away the old putty, using a putty knife, paint thinner, and a scrub pad.

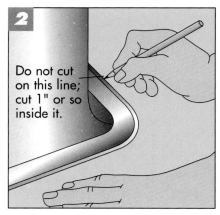

2. Mark the opening.
If you need to cut a new hole, check under the cabinet to make sure there is enough clearance for the sink. The front edge of the sink lip should be 1¾ inches or more from the countertop edge. If your sink comes with a cutting template, tape it on the counter and trace it. If not, place your sink upside down on the countertop. Trace its outline, then draw a line an inch or so to the inside. Erase the first line.

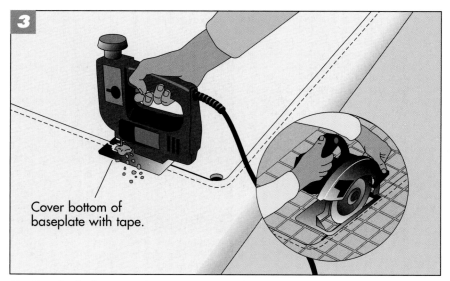

Cover bottom of baseplate with tape.

3. Cut the hole.
To cut into a laminate countertop, drill 1-inch holes at the corners a little inside the line in case of chipping. Cut out the countertop with a sabersaw with a fine-tooth blade. Protect the surface against scratches by covering the baseplate of the saw with electrical or masking tape.

For a tile countertop, use a circular saw with a diamond blade. Cut the tiles slowly and carefully. At the corners, you may have to remove tiles, cut them with a tile cutter, and replace them.

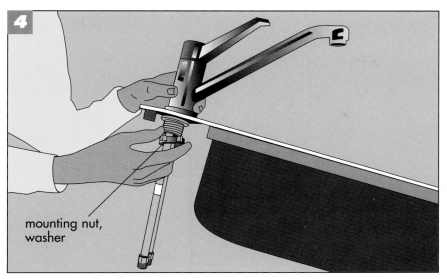

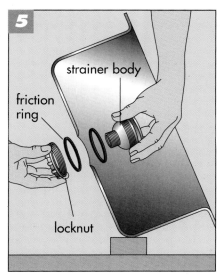

4. Attach the faucet.

Because working under the sink is cramped and unpleasant, it makes sense to attach as many things to the sink as possible before installing it in the countertop.

To install a faucet, either apply a rope of plumber's putty around the three holes or use a gasket provided by the faucet maker. Set the unit in place and tighten the mounting nuts and washers, making sure that the base of the faucet remains aligned correctly.

If you plan to add a spray attachment, an air gap for a dishwasher drain, or a soap dispenser in the fourth hole that comes in most sinks, install them now as well.

5. Connect strainer(s).

Lay a bead of plumber's putty around the sink hole, set the gasket in place, and set the strainer body into the hole. From underneath, slip the friction ring in place and screw on the locknut. Tighten with a spud wrench and clean away the putty that oozes out. You also can attach the tailpiece and trap assembly now (see page 67).

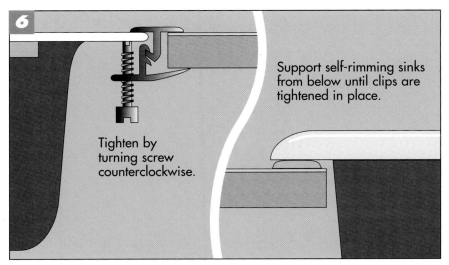

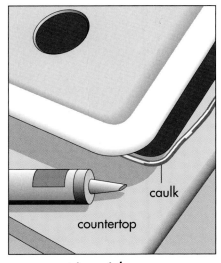

6. Set and secure a steel sink...

To install flush-mounted sinks whose lip sits on a countertop (left), place plumber's putty around the rim so it seals everywhere, including the corners. Turn the sink right side up, and lower it into the opening. Position it so the front lip is parallel to the front of the countertop.

For self-rimming sinks (above), putty the counter and sink edge. Support the sink from underneath and position the rim.

Secure both types of sinks to the countertop with sink clips every 6 to 8 inches, tightening the clips with a screwdriver. Remove excess putty with a putty knife.

...or a cast-iron sink.

Heavier cast-iron sinks do not require clips. Run a bead of silicone sealant under the rim, turn the sink right side up, and set it in place. Wipe away the excess sealant with a rag dipped in paint thinner. Run caulk along the edge and use your finger to make a smooth line.

INSTALLING A NEW FAUCET

Although hundreds of styles of faucets are available, there are few variations in basic design. All kitchen faucets are made to fit the standard three holes, spaced 4 inches apart, found in all sinks. A fourth hole is for a spray unit or other accessories.

Whatever faucet you choose, it will have one of two types of supply connections: flexible copper supply inlets in the center of the unit requiring compression fittings (see Steps 1, 3) or hand-tightened supply hoses located under the hot and cold handles (see Steps 2, 3).

YOU'LL NEED

TIME: A few hours to remove an old faucet and install a new one.
SKILLS: Ability to make fittings in a tight space.
TOOLS: Tongue-and-groove pliers, basin wrench, screwdriver.

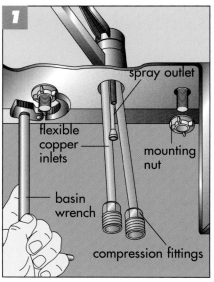

1. Remove the old faucet.
Note: *Shut off the water.* If your faucet has a sprayer, remove the hose from the faucet body. Unhook the supply lines and move them out of the way. Use the basin wrench to remove the mounting nuts holding the faucet to the sink. Lift out the faucet and clean away the old putty.

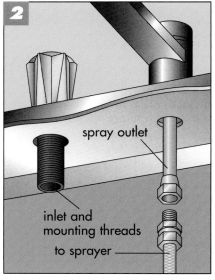

2. Secure the faucet to the sink.
Install a gasket or a rope of plumber's putty beneath the new faucet and set it in place. With a helper holding the unit in position, fasten the mounting nuts and washers. For a sprayer, mount the hose guide and thread the hose through it. Secure the hose to the spray outlet of the faucet.

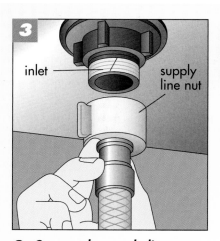

3. Connect the supply lines.
If your lines attach under the handles, brush the inlet threads with pipe joint compound or wrap them with Teflon tape. Twist the supply line nut on and tighten it by hand. Use a basin wrench or pliers to tighten it about a half-turn further—not

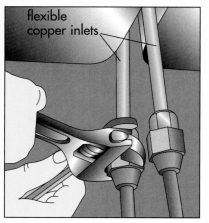

too tight or it might crack. Connect the other end to the shutoff valve in the same way.

If you have flexible copper inlets, take special care not to twist the copper tubes. If they become kinked, the faucet will be ruined. To avoid straining the copper tubes, use two wrenches.

EXPERTS' INSIGHT

INSTALLATION TIPS

■ The hardest part of this job is working in a cramped space under the sink. Make things comfortable. Remove cabinet doors, hook up a work light, and cushion the floor with a drop cloth or towels.
■ If you're installing a sink at the same time as a faucet, attach the faucet to the sink before you install the sink.
■ If old locknuts will not come loose, try penetrating oil. If that doesn't work, tap the nut loose with a hammer and screwdriver.

ADDING A GARDEN WINDOW

A garden window not only lets in light and makes a room seem more spacious, it gives you a place to nurture flowers or herbs right in your kitchen.

Some units have side windows that open casement-style with a crank; the other glass pieces are fixed in place. Prices vary widely, depending on whether you prefer a vinyl, metal, or wood unit. Some manufacturers offer off-the-shelf units made to standard window dimensions; others produce made-to-measure units only.

YOU'LL NEED

TIME: 1 day to remove a window and add a garden window.
SKILLS: Demolition, measuring, cutting, sealing.
TOOLS: Hammer, flat pry bar, reciprocating saw or metal-cutting keyhole saw, drill, caulking gun, level.

MEASUREMENTS

DETERMINING THE ROUGH OPENING

Garden windows often are not in stock, so you'll need accurate measurements of the rough opening (without removing the old window) to place an order. Here are some hints:

■ If you have old double-hung sash windows with ropes (or chains) attached to weights in the side cavities, measure from jamb to jamb (the surfaces that the sides of the sash slide against) and add 5 inches.

■ For newer-style windows, measure the casing (the molding that is on the wall) from outside edge to outside edge, and subtract 3 inches.

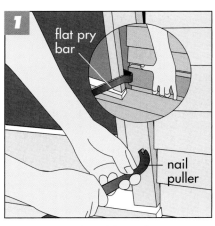

flat pry bar

nail puller

1. Remove the old window.
Use a hammer and flat pry bar to pull off the molding, both inside and outside. On the sides and at the top, you will be able to look through your wall. You'll see a series of nails holding the window in place. Cut the nails with a reciprocating saw or metal-cutting keyhole saw, or chop them in two by chiseling through them with the pry bar and hammer. Remove the window.

1× spacer to fit out opening

2. Measure, fill in.
The directions accompanying your window will tell you what the size of the rough opening should be. Cut away framing pieces only if you know how to reframe the opening in keeping with local codes. Make the opening smaller by filling in the space with 1× or 2× spacers. Allow about ½ inch of wiggle room on all sides of the garden window—you can shim the difference later.

3. Install the window.
Tip the garden window into place, making sure the front edge is flush with the wall surface so the molding will sit flat. Level and plumb, then firmly anchor it to the framing with shims and screws. On the outside, apply generous beads of exterior caulk before covering over the seam with molding. If your new window is a good deal smaller than the old one, you may need to use extra-wide molding (see inset). This is a simpler solution than filling in exterior siding or masonry.

BATHROOM REMODELING

Second only to the kitchen in complexity, bathrooms present many remodeling challenges. You often have to make the most of limited space, and you usually have the expense and trouble of upgrading plumbing fixtures and fittings. In addition, a bathroom remodeling may require repairs to rotted floors and spongy walls before installing new tile or other surface finishes.

Moisture always is an issue in bathrooms. Whether you're trying to remove it by adding ventilation, tracking down a small leak ruining the ceiling in the room below, or adding a new ceramic tile floor to cope with the splish-splash of a family-size quota of daily showers, one of the main goals of a bathroom remodeling should be to keep water where it belongs.

Often, space constraints won't permit moving walls to enlarge a bathroom. The only recourse is to revamp the floor plan to use space as wisely as possible to meet household needs. (See pages 58–59 for ideas about developing floor plans.)

The examples on these pages show how smart planning and the careful choice of materials can transform even modest-size bathrooms. As with a kitchen remodeling, the improvements added in a bath makeover will be appreciated every day. Here are some ideas for doing the job right.

ABOVE: You can use color to add a new variation on an old theme. Rich molding, beadboard wainscotting, vintage tile, and an old tub well worth preserving combine to provide the setting for new fixtures in an old style. Only the punch of fresh color belies this bathroom's transformation. Otherwise, it looks unchanged by time.

RIGHT: Make the best of limited space. Two doorways ate up too much useable space in the earlier incarnation of this bathroom. Eliminating one door allowed the tub and toilet to switch places. The shapely lines of a new window are echoed in a new wall-hung lavatory that provides extra inches of precious floor space.

RIGHT: If you discovered a successful approach when making over your kitchen, you may want to repeat it in the bathroom. The same marble used in the kitchen makes a big impression in this master bathroom. Any surface that may fall victim to a splash can be an opportunity for decoration with a permanent material like stone or ceramic tile.

As part of a Victorian house, this bathroom was planned so up-to-the-minute innovations, such as the whirlpool bathtub, would fit in with nary a ripple. Understated colors mean many a year will roll by without this carefully crafted room looking dated.

LEFT: Make space for display. A built-in set of shelves for plants and collectibles was installed in otherwise wasted wall space. The traditional vanity, snugged up against the tiled enclosure of the whirlpool tub, takes advantage of every inch of available space. This bathroom is part of a master suite, so one of the sinks was fitted with a filtered hot water dispenser for making coffee or tea.

Ample storage was planned to keep the bathroom clutter free. Cabinets above the vanity counter were fitted with electrical receptacles so hair dryers, shavers, and other personal appliances could be plugged in where they are stored—handy to use but not constantly in sight.

A deep whirlpool tub provides a leisurely place to soak. Because one of the homeowners likes to read in the bath they installed a ceiling light above it.

LEFT: *Plan for neutral surfaces that allow innovation. The straightforward tile treatment in this bath is an ideal backdrop for accents, such as the ladder towel rack and the Indian sari used as a shower curtain. Good design, easily maintained surfaces, and plenty of natural light add up to a utilitarian bath that doesn't scrimp on good looks. The homeowner's prescription for success: Determine your needs in advance, research product choices carefully, and don't hesitate to draw on the expertise of everyone from manufacturers' representatives to local craftspeople.*

BELOW: *Blending nostalgia and economy, the best features of a shabby and antiquated bath were preserved in this refined but still antique-looking makeover. Fortunately, the bath was still plumbed with its original claw-foot tub and pedestal sink—fixtures that people restoring old homes often spend lots of effort and expense to get. Both were refinished. The tile floor and wainscotting are new; the medicine cabinet got new hardware and paint.*

RIGHT: *If you need plenty of storage space, you can make it decorative as well. An ample vanity and dual medicine cabinets make this sink area a hard-working, good-looking asset to the bath.*

BELOW LEFT: *Complement up-to-the-minute architecture with old-world features. Although often pricey, reproduction fixtures, such as this console sink, can be eye-catching centerpieces. Combined with reproduction light fixtures, faucets, and vintage tile, the result is understated elegance.*

BELOW RIGHT: *Put limited space and pleasing angles to good use. This small, under-the-rafters bathroom has headroom only where absolutely needed. During remodeling, the owners refinished an old tub, echoed the style of light fixtures found elsewhere in the house, and selected a classic tile pattern for the floor.*

PLANNING A BATHROOM

Bathrooms are small, but they're densely packed with potential projects. In fact, most of the installations needed for a kitchen also are needed in a bathroom.

Begin by assessing your needs:
■ Do you want privacy, or should two people be able to use the bathroom at the same time?
■ Do you want the basic ensemble of toilet, tub/shower, and sink, or would you like something extra, such as a spa, a double sink, or a luxury shower?
■ Do you need more light? If you have a window, is it in a place where water collects and causes problems?
■ Do you need better ventilation, another electrical outlet, more counter space around the sink or at other places?
■ Do you have enough towel racks and other storage room?
■ Is the shower or tub large enough?
■ What style is your bath calling out for?

If you examine your present bathroom, you may be surprised at how much of it can be salvaged. If the basic layout works—the fixtures are placed comfortably apart and there is enough room left for storage and towel racks— then you can keep your basic plumbing and only replace fixtures. Even if your bathroom as a whole looks depressing, one or more of the fixtures may have a place in a new, fresh-looking bathroom. Not all old-fashioned wall or floor tiles may have to be replaced. Perhaps you can find new fixtures, tiles, and wall treatments to go with them.

If you do decide to move fixtures around, be prepared for major plumbing chores. The first question to ask is whether you can run a drain to the new fixture location. You may need to hire a professional plumber to tell you if you need to install a new plumbing vent—a major project (see pages 86–91).

If the space seems unworkable, consider moving walls to make more room. See pages 58–59 for some examples.

Lighting is important in a bathroom. Usually, you want a good general overhead light, another overhead light in the tub area, and lights above or alongside the medicine cabinet and mirror. Choose these carefully. You should aim for adequate illumination without glare.

Minimum Allowance for Bathroom Fixtures

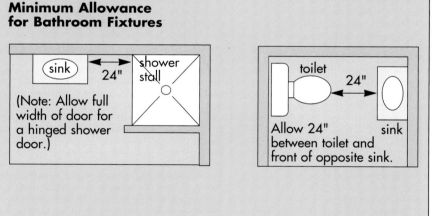

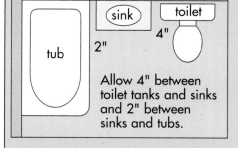

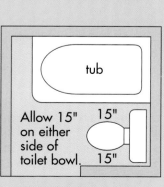

Arrange fixtures with sufficient clearance in mind.
When it comes to bathroom fixtures, an inch or two can make the difference between feeling comfortable or cramped. Map out the floor of your bathroom on graph paper. Cut out scale-size pieces of paper to represent the fixtures. Move the pieces around until you find the most usable configuration. If a door swings inward, make sure it won't bump into a fixture or built-in unit.

The dimensions given in these drawings show the minimum requirements for ease of use. Fixtures placed closer to each other than these minimums will make you feel squeezed. Usually, it's best to give yourself more room than the minimum, but don't go overboard and space things too far apart. Watch the details: Plan your towel racks at the same time as you plan your fixtures.

PLANNING CHECKLIST

When planning a bathroom remodel, don't forget these essential elements:
- Basic plumbing, including vented drains for all fixtures; hot and cold supplies for tub/shower and for sink; cold supply for toilet
- Bathtub or shower stall
- Tub and shower faucet
- Wall-hung, pedestal, or vanity-installed sink
- Toilet
- Lighting: overhead, medicine cabinet
- Electrical receptacles
- Vent fan and ductwork
- Heat
- Paint or wallpaper for walls and ceiling
- Tiles or sheeting around tub, on shower walls
- Countertops
- Cabinets and shelves
- Towel racks and hooks
- Space for the bathroom scale

Money $ Saver

SPENDING LESS ON A BATH REMODEL

A spanking new bathroom with all new fixtures and tiles can cost as much as some new cars if you buy top-of-the-line products and hire someone to do the work. Here are some ways to cut costs:
- You may find the tile you want on a closeout special. Often stores slash prices when they have less than 50 square feet of a style remaining—plenty for most bathrooms. Instead of buying expensive wall tiles, you may opt for a custom look by using two or more colors of less-expensive tiles.
- Consider going for a vintage look. It may take some shopping around, but an ensemble of old, used fixtures can look great and cost far less than high-end new products.
- Do at least some of the work yourself. Even if you need a plumber to rough in the drains and supplies, you may be able to save significant amounts by doing the finish work yourself.

CHOOSING A SINK

STYLES

- Pedestal sinks add a splash of style to bathrooms and styles range from antique reproductions to sleek contemporary. Because they take up little space, they work well in small rooms. On the down side, they don't have the storage or counter space of vanities.
- Use a wall-hung sink if you need to save space. It has the same disadvantages of a pedestal sink; it also reveals all the plumbing.
- A vanity takes up floor space, but provides useful counter and storage space. The usual arrangement involves a one-piece sink/counter that sits on a vanity. It's the easiest type of sink to install.

MATERIALS

- Vitreous china is easy to clean. Its gleaming surface can be maintained with little bother.
- Enameled cast-iron sinks are durable, but are heavy and often expensive.
- Polymer or fiberglass-reinforced plastic sinks are almost impossible to crack or chip, but lose their shine in time.
- Simulated or cultured marble surfaces give you a classy look for a small amount of money, but they are susceptible to scratches and nicks.

CHOOSING A TUB

TYPES

- A standard tub is 60 inches long and about 30 inches wide. (If you are replacing a tub, make sure the new one will cover your flooring—it may be an inch or so narrower.) A tub fits into one side wall and two end walls. You can also buy 54-inch models.
- Consider a small spa that fits into the space of a tub. Choose one with fully adjustable hydrojets. Larger spas need to be framed around and tiled.
- Old-fashioned claw-foot tubs still can be purchased. Because all the plumbing will be visible, you may want to purchase special pipes and fittings.

MATERIALS

- Enameled cast iron is the best tub material, but it is expensive and so heavy you may need to hire a professional to install it. It retains heat well, cleans easily, and muffles sounds.
- An enameled steel tub costs and weighs less, but is substantially lower in quality. Not only will the water turn cold quickly, but it makes a tinny sound when water runs in it, and the finish will chip easily.
- Acrylic, fiberglass, or polymer tubs will not crack, and they hold heat well. The better models hold their shine fairly well, but not as long as cast iron.

EXPANDING INTO A CLOSET

Often you can enlarge a bathroom or install a new powder room by stealing space from a nearby closet or bedroom.

The complexity of changing the layout of your bathroom varies depending on which fixtures you move and where the plumbing needs to go.

Start your plans by locating the wet wall—the wall containing the waste stack and other plumbing pipes. If you position the new fixtures along or close to the wet wall, you will save money in plumbing and demolition. In most cases, sinks are much easier to move than toilets or tubs.

If you plan on removing part of a wall, make sure it does not support the roof or walls on the floors above it. If it is load-bearing, you can remove it only if you position a beam to handle the job it used to do. Partition walls—those supporting no weight above—can be removed without concern about weakening the structure. With both types of walls you may have to reroute plumbing or wiring.

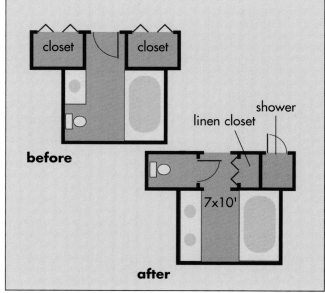

Move a toilet and add a shower and linen closet.
Moving the toilet and adding a shower stall and a second sink makes this bathroom usable by more than one person at a time. Installing a set of bifold doors and some shelves provides a handy closet for towels and bathroom supplies.

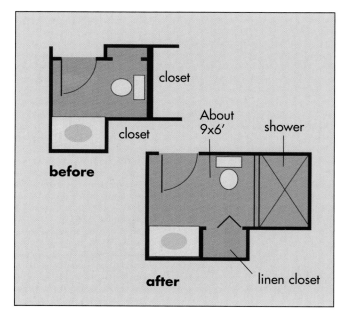

Add a shower stall.
By taking over an adjacent closet, a powder room can be made into a full bath. The shower is extra large—3½×4½ feet. A new linen closet is handy for both the sink and the shower.

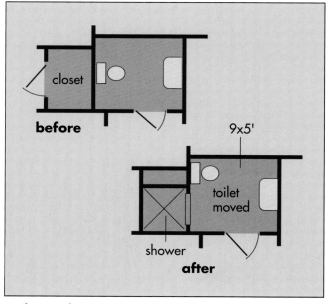

Tuck in a shower.
This is about as small as a full bathroom can get without becoming claustrophobic. Moving the toilet just a few feet made space for the shower door.

SQUEEZING IN A POWDER ROOM

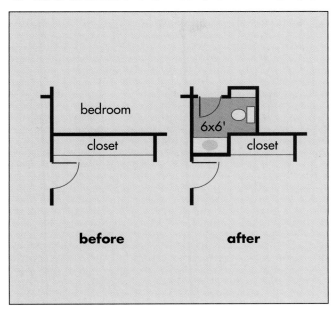

Use bedroom space.
A chunk of space from a large bedroom was used to make this small powder room. The sink sits in an alcove made by using part of the closet in the adjoining room.

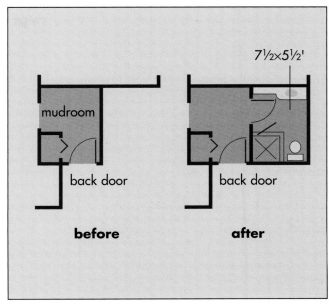

Add space on.
A small addition to this house provided just enough space for a powder room with a shower stall, making it a three-quarter bathroom. Only two exterior walls needed to be built, but a new plumbing vent had to be installed.

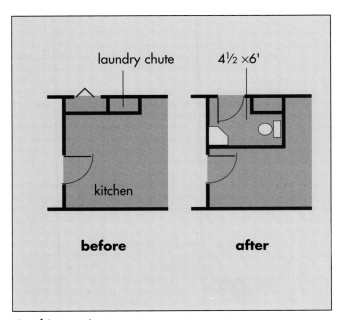

Combine projects.
Demolition work for a kitchen remodeling left plumbing exposed. As long as all that dust was being created, it made sense to go ahead and install a modest powder room.

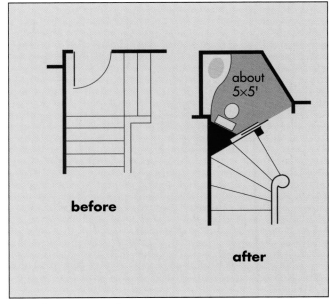

Search out unusual space.
You don't want a powder room with a door that looks directly into a living or dining room. This trapezoidal room on the upper landing of the basement steps offers privacy, but easy access from the first floor.

TILING A TUB SURROUND

If the tiles around your tub area are buckling or falling off, remove a section of tile and examine the wall behind them. Before you replace the tiles, you need to patch any damaged wall surface and rotted framing. It's likely the damage resulted from water seeping through gaps in the grout or caulk—things you will fix when you retile. But if there is another place where water can seep in, for example, cracked or rotting wood around a window, be sure to repair and seal it or you will have to do this job over again soon. Spend a little extra to use cement board, which is longer-lasting than green drywall, for the tile backing.

If a bathroom window has wooden moldings and jambs, consider tearing out or cutting back the moldings and trimming the window with tiles instead. You even can cover part of the jambs with tile. To eliminate the problems of a wooden window altogether, install glass block (see pages 62–63).

When you buy wall tiles, show the salesperson your plan. Make sure you have all the pieces: field tiles, bullnose pieces (caps), and any decorative pieces you choose to add.

YOU'LL NEED

TIME: Once the walls are repaired, most of a day to tile, and a few hours the next day to grout the tiles.
SKILLS: Measuring and cutting tile, laying out a level and straight field of tiles.
TOOLS: Level, tile cutter, nibbling tool or hacksaw with ceramic cutting blade, rasp or abrasive stone, tile-cutting holesaw, notched trowel, grout float, sponge, chalk line.

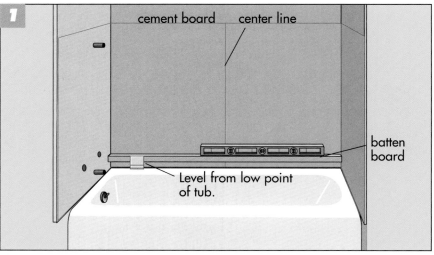

1. Prepare the surface, lay out.
Repair the walls or install new cement board. If your walls are straight and smooth and the end walls are square to the tub, tiling will be easier.

Establish a vertical working line by laying the tiles in a row on the tub and making sure there will be the same size tile on each end or there will not be any narrow

2. Lay the field tiles.
Apply the mastic with the correct-sized notched trowel and set the tiles, giving each a little twist and push to make sure they stick. Start with the row sitting on the batten. Most wall tiles are self-spacing. Once you have several rows installed, remove the batten and install the bottom row.

pieces. If the end walls are out of square with the tub, factor in how the pieces will change size as you move upward.

To establish a horizontal working line, measure up the height of one tile from the low point of the tub. Draw a level line at that point. Then tack a straight batten board along its length to use as a guide board.

CAUTION!
PROTECT YOUR TUB AND DRAIN
Tiling creates abrasive debris. Sharp chips from cut tile will fall into the tub. If you repair the wall first, you will produce plaster and other debris. Without protection, you'll scratch the tub and clog the drain. Refinished tubs or drains that run slowly already are particularly susceptible. To protect the tub, don't just throw a drop cloth over it. That can make matters worse by trapping particles underneath it. Buy a special tub cover or tape red rosin paper (the pink protective paper contractors use) to cover the tub. To avoid clogs, stick a rag firmly in the drain so no debris can go down it.

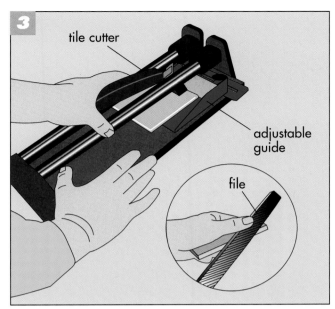

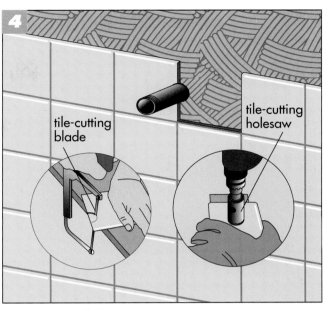

3. Cut tiles to fit.
Use a standard tile cutter for the straight cuts. Hold the tile in place on the wall and mark it for cutting. Set the tile on the cutter and score the surface by bearing down and sliding the cutter once. Break off the piece by pushing down on the handle. For a series of tiles all cut to the same size, use the adjustable guide found on most cutters. Smooth the ragged cut edges with a file, rasp, or abrasive stone.

4. Cut around pipes.
Cuts around pipes do not have to be exact because they will be covered by escutcheons. Use a nibbling tool or pliers to slowly eat away a curved cut (see page 40). Or cut it with a hacksaw equipped with a tile-cutting blade. To cut a hole in the middle of a tile, use a tile-cutting holesaw. Or set the tile on scrap wood and drill a series of closely spaced holes with a masonry bit, then carefully tap out the hole.

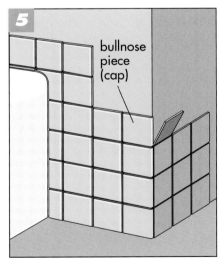

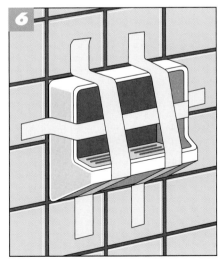

5. Install end and corner pieces.
Use special bullnose pieces (also called caps) everywhere there will be an exposed edge. (Do not try to use a field tile and grout—it will look sloppy.) Although difficult to find, you also can use special corner pieces that have two bullnose edges.

6. Attach accessories.
Apply adhesive and use masking tape to hold soap dishes and other accessories in place until they are set. You can take the tape off after a day or two and apply grout, but wait a week or so for the adhesive to set up completely before using the accessory.

7. Grout, wipe, and buff.
Mix the grout and push it into the joints with a grout float held nearly flat. Then tip the float up and wipe away excess grout. Carefully wipe the surface to produce consistent grout lines. You may want to tool the surface with the handle of a toothbrush. Wipe several times. Finally, buff with a dry cloth.

INSTALLING A GLASS BLOCK WINDOW

A glass block window is more resistant to moisture than most windows, and it provides fairly good insulation. When replacing an existing window, remove the jamb as well as the window. Pry away all the shims and spacers so the glass blocks can be joined directly to the framing of the house or a masonry surface.

You may want to install glass block when you tile your bath. Tile and glass block make an easy-to-maintain wall that is impervious to water damage.

YOU'LL NEED

TIME: 1 day to install blocks in a medium-sized window.
SKILLS: Measuring, laying out blocks, working with mortar.
TOOLS: Mason's trowel, sled jointer or joint strike, diagonal cutting pliers, drill.

Money $ Saver

ORDER A PREFABRICATED GLASS BLOCK WINDOW

The easiest way to install a glass block window is to measure your opening carefully (make allowances if it is not square), then order a pre-assembled unit from a supplier who specializes in glass block.

The unit will be made of blocks mortared together, then banded together firmly with a metal strap. It will be extremely heavy if the window is more than a couple of feet square. To install the whole unit, you simply lay a bed of mortar on the sill, set the glass block unit in place, and fill in mortar all around.

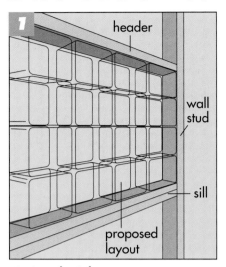

1. Lay the job out.
Measure the opening and choose the type of block to use—there are several sizes available. If your opening is not square, plan on a combination of blocks that will fit inside a rectangular space. You may have to alter the size of the rough opening. Replace rotted framing pieces surrounding the window. Make sure the sill is solid.

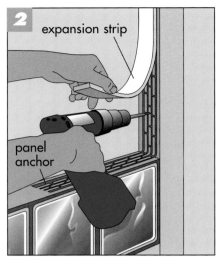

2. Install anchors, jamb strips.
Determine where your joint lines will be along the jambs. Screw panel anchors to the side jambs every few courses and install expansion strips between the anchors along the frame.

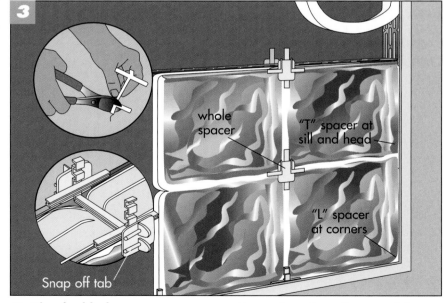

3. Plan for block spacers.
Do a dry run of a few blocks to become familiar with when and how to trim and install spacers. Use whole spacers for places where four blocks meet. Using diagonal cutting pliers, modify spacers to T and L shapes for use at the bottom and top of the window and at the corners. The outer tab of the whole spacer twists off after the mortar has set.

EXPERTS' INSIGHT

GLASS BLOCK TIPS

■ Because glass block does not soak up moisture like bricks or concrete blocks, the mortar should be much dryer than that used for laying bricks. However, it shouldn't be so dry that it won't stick to the block.

■ Mortar is much harder to clean after it has set, so clean up as you go. Check the mortar in the joints for stiffness after laying every four or five blocks. Because you are starting with fairly dry mortar, you may need to strike some joints before you have set all the blocks in place.

■ Check each row for level. It's easy to forget a spacer or to have one twist, so make sure each row is straight before going on to the next.

4. Lay the first row.
Lay a bed of mortar on the sill and begin laying blocks. Butter the blocks as you would for a brick wall. Do not apply mortar to the edges that touch the jamb strips. Use spacers to maintain consistent joint lines. (See *Better Homes and Gardens® Step-By-Step Masonry & Concrete* for instructions on handling and applying mortar.)

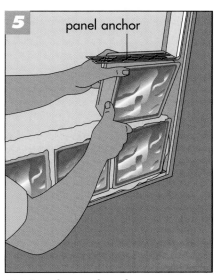

5. Attach panel anchors.
Every third course or so you will run into a panel anchor. The top of the block—including the spacer—should fit just under the anchor. If necessary, adjust the height of the anchor by adjusting the screws holding it to the jamb. Once the row is completed, spread mortar over the panel anchor just as with regular blocks.

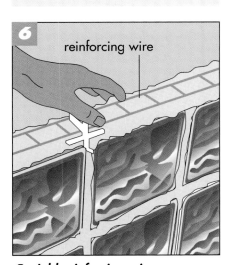

6. Add reinforcing wire.
Every two or three courses, press galvanized reinforcing wire into the mortar bed on top of the course of blocks. Trim pieces to fit with diagonal cutting pliers. If you need more than one length, overlap the pieces by at least 6 inches.

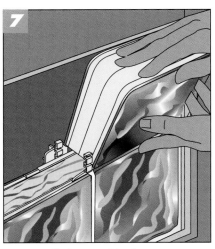

7. Install the top blocks.
The tops of the top blocks need no mortar because they meet an expansion strip at the head. Place the L spacers in position as you install the corner blocks and the T spacers when installing the other blocks in between.

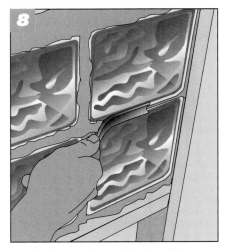

8. Strike and caulk both sides.
Make smooth and consistent joints by running a joint strike along the horizontal lines first, then the vertical lines. Wipe away excess mortar and repeat as often as needed. After the mortar is firm, apply a thick bead of caulk around the perimeter of the window. You can install molding around the window as well.

INSTALLING AN EXHAUST FAN/LIGHT

An efficient exhaust fan removes moisture and odor from your bathroom, protecting walls from mildew and rot. It dehumidifies your house and even can lower air-conditioning costs. If your bathroom does not have a window that opens, most building codes require a vent fan. You can wire a bathroom fan so it operates by itself, but some codes require the fan to come on when you switch on the light.

YOU'LL NEED

TIME: About a day, assuming easy access to ceiling cavities.
SKILLS: Fishing wire, making electrical connections, cutting through walls.
TOOLS: Screwdriver, lineman's pliers, drill, reciprocating saw or keyhole saw.

MEASUREMENTS

WILL IT REALLY VENT?

Many bathroom fans do little more than make noise because they lack the power to draw moisture through the ductwork to the outside. The larger the room and the longer the duct, the more powerful the fan needs to be. When you shop for a ventilation fan, know the size of your bathroom (height as well as floor area) and how long the ducting will be. If the salesperson cannot help you choose the right size fan, check the manufacturer's directions.

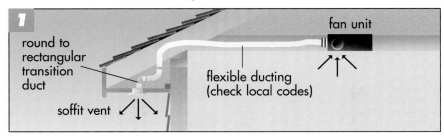

1. Run the ductwork.
In most regions, you need to vent outside, rather than into an attic cavity. Check local codes. Run flexible ducting to a soffit, straight out the wall, or to a roof-mounted vent (see page 20). For greatest efficiency, run the ducts as straight as possible. Solid ducts are more efficient than flexible ducts.

flush with surface of ceiling

2. Install the fan unit.
Note: *Shut off the power.* Cut a ceiling opening between joists. From the attic, if possible, nail or screw the unit's mounting brackets securely to the framing. Make sure the fan assembly is level and flush with the surface of the ceiling before fastening it.

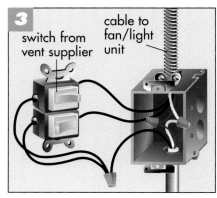

3. Wire the switches.
For a combination fan and light, fish two-wire cable to the switches, then run three-wire cable from the switches to the unit. For a fan only, run two-wire cable. If the fan has a heater, you'll need a separate 15- or 20-amp circuit. See pages 92–97 for wiring basics.

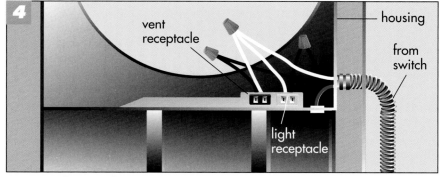

4. Wire the vent fan.
Inside the unit, connect the wires according to manufacturer's directions. Typical connections are shown above. Install the working parts in the housing and plug them into the appropriate receptacles. Turn on the power and test the fan and light. Finally, fit the grille. Once a year, clean the fan blades and other parts inside the fan housing.

INSTALLING A VANITY

Vanities are popular because they add much-needed storage in otherwise wasted space. In addition, a vanity sink is easier to install than a wall-hung or pedestal unit. The rough plumbing does not have to be positioned precisely because the vanity will cover up the pipes and lines. For information about running the supplies and drain, see pages 86–91. For the simplest installation and maintenance, choose a top with the sink and counter molded in one piece.

YOU'LL NEED
TIME: Half a day to remove the old sink and install a vanity.
SKILLS: Making plumbing connections, leveling.
TOOLS: Pipe wrench, tongue-and-groove pliers, drill, screwdriver, level, hacksaw, sabersaw or keyhole saw.

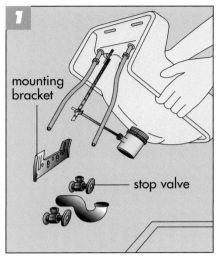

3. Install the sink top.
Install the faucet, flexible supply lines, and drain assembly on the sink. Set the sink on top of the cabinet. Make sure it is centered with the backsplash tight against the wall. Attach the sink to the vanity. Connect the drain trap and the supply lines. Run a bead of caulk where the backsplash meets the wall.

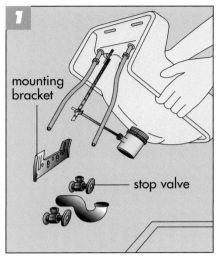

1. Remove the old sink.
Note: *Shut off the water supply.*
If you have an old wall-hung sink, disconnect the trap and the supply lines. Cut away the caulk sealing the sink to the wall. With some models, you simply can lift them up and away. Others are connected to the mounting brackets with bolts, which probably will be rusted. Use penetrating oil or cut through them with a hacksaw.

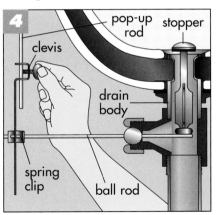

4. Connect pop-up assembly.
Insert the ball rod into the opening and secure it with the nut. Slip the rod through the clevis strap and secure it with the spring clip. Lower the pop-up rod down through the hole in the faucet spout. Slide on the clevis strap and tighten lightly. Adjust the clevis so the stopper seals when the rod is pulled up. Tighten the screw.

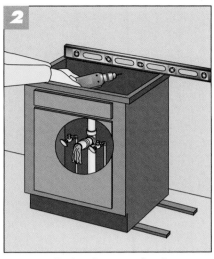

2. Install plumbing and cabinet.
Install new stop valves and a drain line, making sure they will be covered by the cabinet and won't interfere with the sink. If the cabinet has a back, measure and cut out holes for the pipes. Slide the cabinet into position and level it in both directions, using shims if necessary. Anchor it to the wall by driving screws through the cabinet frame and into the wall studs.

EXPERTS' INSIGHT

CHOOSING A VANITY AND SINK
■ A larger vanity is worth the cost if you have the space. It provides usable counter space and a larger bowl, as well as more storage space below.
■ Choose an integral sink and countertop for the easiest installation. Most are heavy enough so you need only a bead of caulk underneath to attach the countertop to the cabinet.
■ Vitreous china is expensive and chips easily, and fiberglass or plastic materials get dull with time. Synthetic marble is one of the best choices for a top.

INSTALLING A PEDESTAL SINK

Installing a pedestal sink is an inexpensive way to make a stylish addition to a bathroom. However, because the pedestal hugs the wall to hide the plumbing, installation is more difficult than for a vanity or a wall-hung sink. You'll need to position all the plumbing to fit behind the pedestal and attach the sink at the right height so the pedestal slides in underneath. Less-expensive units often have narrow pedestals, making installation more difficult.

YOU'LL NEED

TIME: A day to move the plumbing and install the sink.
SKILLS: Basic plumbing and carpentry skills.
TOOLS: Keyhole or reciprocating saw, hammer or drill, screwdriver, tongue-and-groove pliers, adjustable and socket wrenches.

EXPERTS' INSIGHT

WHAT WILL SHOW?

■ Set up your pedestal sink in its future location to get a clear idea if you will be able to hide all the plumbing. It may take careful planning to keep everything covered.
■ You may decide to let some of the plumbing show. In that case, buy decorative stops, supply lines, and drain pieces. Use solid brass or paint the pipes using an alcohol-based primer. You still need to position the water supply stops carefully so they and the sink form a symmetrical ensemble.

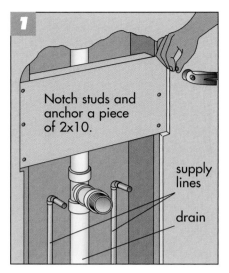

Notch studs and anchor a piece of 2x10.

supply lines

drain

1. Rough in, provide bracing.
Note: *Shut off the water and drain the water lines.* If you need to remove an old sink, see page 65. Measure carefully when installing new plumbing or moving the lines to ensure they will be covered by the pedestal. Provide solid framing for the hanger bracket.

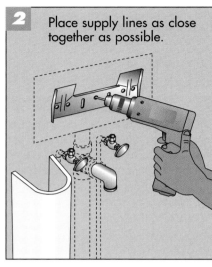

Place supply lines as close together as possible.

2. Install the bracket.
Patch the wall, then prime and paint it and allow it to dry for at least a day. Carefully measure the position of the bracket. Set the sink on its pedestal to confirm the height is correct. Check for level and attach the bracket by driving screws into the 2×10 brace.

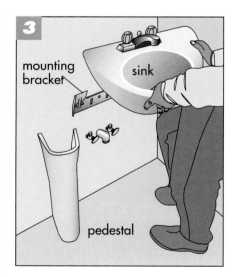

mounting bracket

sink

pedestal

3. Attach sink, connect plumbing.
Install the faucet and pop-up drain assembly on the sink (see page 65). Set the sink on the bracket and temporarily slide the base in place to make sure it is at the correct height. Remove the pedestal and connect the drain and supply lines. Restore the water pressure and check for leaks.

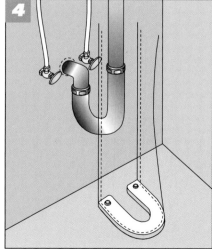

4. Install the pedestal.
Slide the pedestal base in under the sink. For some models, you have to attach it to the floor with bolts. If the pedestal does not sit flat on the floor, run a bead of silicone caulk under it; wipe away excess caulk so it is not visible.

INSTALLING A WALL-HUNG SINK

Wall-hung sinks are not as popular as they once were, but are worth considering where space is limited or a retro style is called for. The plumbing underneath will be visible, so make it symmetrical and consider buying chromium-plated supply lines, stop valves, and drain assembly. A sink like this will last a long time under normal use, but warn family members not to sit on it. It could crack or pull away from the wall.

YOU'LL NEED

TIME: Half a day to add framing and finish the wall; about 2 hours to hang the sink.
SKILLS: Basic plumbing and carpentry skills.
TOOLS: Keyhole or reciprocating saw, level, screwdriver, tongue-and-groove pliers, adjustable wrench.

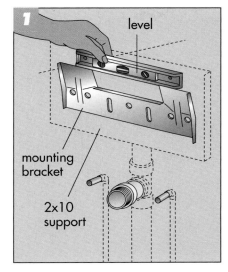

1. Install bracing, bracket.
Note: *Shut off the water.* Remove the old sink. If necessary, install bracing in the wall as shown on page 66. Install stop valves if there are none. Patch the wall, prime, and paint. Allow a day for the paint to dry. Level and attach the mounting bracket with screws.

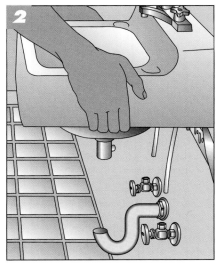

2. Set the sink in place.
Attach the faucet, flexible supply lines, and the pop-up assembly to the sink. Carefully, so as not to damage the paint on the wall, hold the sink flat against the wall and lower it onto the bracket. Push down so it seats completely. The bracket flange fits into a corresponding slot in the sink.

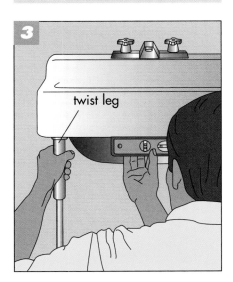

3. Attach the legs.
If the sink has support legs, insert them into the holes in the bottom of the sink, check them for plumb, and adjust them so they firmly support the sink. To do this, twist the top portion of each leg. Check that the sink is level.

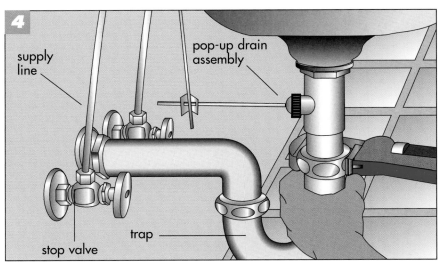

4. Hook up supplies, drain.
Connect the flexible supply lines to the stop valves. Attach the trap to the sink drain and to the drain pipe. Adjust the pop-up drain assembly so the stopper seals when the rod is up (see page 65). Restore the water pressure and check supply lines for leaks. To test the drain for leaks, pull the stopper lever up, fill the bowl, and open the stopper. Once the sink is completely plumbed and firmly in place, you may want to run a bead of silicone caulk where the sink meets the wall.

ADDING A TILED SINK TOP

This project takes some time and patience. But the result can be a sink top that adds an appealing custom touch to your makeover and melds with the tile surfaces in your bathroom.

Begin with an off-the-shelf cabinet base or, if you are an experienced woodworker, make one yourself. Select the sink, faucet, and grout at the same time as you buy the tiles so you have a grouping that goes well together. Avoid choosing a pigmented grout of a color that contrasts strongly with the tiles.

YOU'LL NEED:

TIME: A day to build the substrate and lay the tiles, another hour the next day to grout the tiles.
SKILLS: Basic carpentry skills, measuring and cutting tiles.
TOOLS: Circular saw and sabersaw, drill, hammer, screwdriver, notched trowel, tile cutter, caulking gun, grout float, sponge.

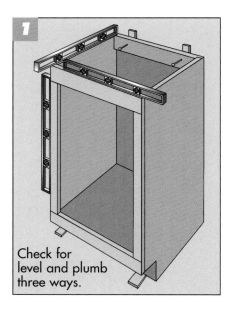

Check for level and plumb three ways.

1. Install the cabinet.

If not already in place, install a drain line and supply lines with stop valves. Cut holes in the back of the cabinet for the pipes and slide the cabinet into place. Shim where necessary to ensure the cabinet is plumb and level. Attach it to the wall by driving screws through the cabinet framing and into wall studs.

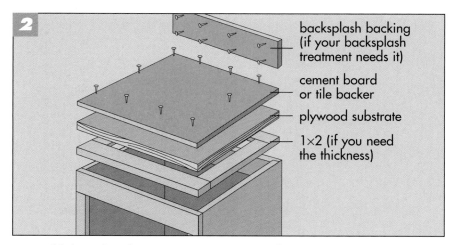

backsplash backing (if your backsplash treatment needs it)

cement board or tile backer

plywood substrate

1×2 (if you need the thickness)

2. Build the subsurface.

The surface under your tiles must be perfectly flat and smooth, and the edges and backsplash piece should be the correct sizes to accommodate the bullnose tile. If possible, plan the subsurface so you'll use as many whole tiles as possible to eliminate cutting tiles.

Cut $3/4$-inch plywood to the size needed. To build out a base for the tiled edge, fasten 1×2 pieces around the perimeter with glue and screws. On top of the plywood, add a piece of cement board or tile backer. Attach it with screws. Make sure their heads are all driven below the surface.

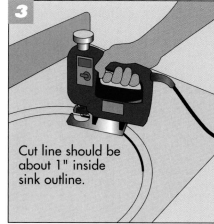

Cut line should be about 1" inside sink outline.

3. Cut the hole.

The sink manufacturer may supply a template for marking the cutout. If not, center the sink upside-down on the top and draw an outline. Draw a second line, about an inch inside the first and cut on that line using a sabersaw.

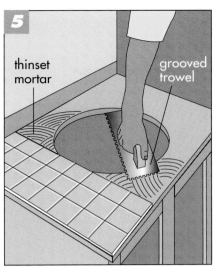

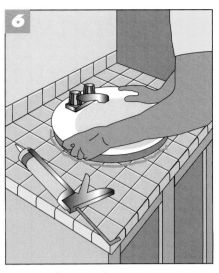

4. Make a dry run.

Dry-lay the tiles out in the exact position where you want them. When laying out the edge pieces, remember that the mortar will be about ⅛ inch thick. (For cutting the tiles, see page 40.) Set the sink in place to make sure no tile edges will be visible.

5. Apply mastic, tile.

Remove the tiles and set them down so you can remember where all of them go. Apply mastic—thinset mortar is a good choice—with a notched trowel. First lay it on thickly, then comb it with the trowel notches for a perfectly level surface. Push the tiles into the mastic as you place them. Use the spacers (see page 41) to maintain consistent joint lines.

6. Install the sink.

After the mastic sets up, grout the tiles and allow the grout to dry (see page 41). Set the sink in place and make the plumbing connections (see pages 65 and 67). If the sink has attaching clamps, install and tighten them; heavy sinks do not require clamps. Run a bead of silicone caulk around the rim. Smooth the caulk with a rag soaked with paint thinner.

Removing old sinks.

Rimmed sinks usually are easy to remove. Unhook the plumbing connections, disconnect mounting clips (if any) from underneath, cut the bead of caulk, and pull it up.

Use a couple of pieces of 2×4 and a piece of rope to support a flush-mounted sink as you remove the clamps holding it in place.

Otherwise, the sink may fall down into the cabinet.

A recessed sink, which sits under the countertop surface (usually tiles), is held on with special mounting clamps. If they are rusted, use penetrating oil before unscrewing them. If you cannot turn the countertop upside-down, as shown, be sure to

support the sink as you remove it.

If you want to keep the old tiles and your new sink will be large enough to fit in the old hole, carefully chip away the old quarter-round tiles that cover the top of a recessed sink so the surface tiles are preserved. Then install the new sink and replace the quarter-round tiles.

ADDING A WHIRLPOOL TUB

Here we show how to install the simplest type of whirlpool tub, one that fits into a 5-foot opening and has a removable apron covering the length of the tub on one side. If you want to install a regular tub, use the same instructions, skipping the steps that do not apply. For a whirlpool tub with more than one exposed side, see page 71 for general instructions on framing around it.

Many whirlpools are built so you can remove a standard tub and slide in the whirlpool with a minimum of alterations. The supply and drain lines will match up, and you may be able to save the wall tiles. However, measure carefully before purchasing and make sure the new tub covers as much of the floor as needed.

A cast-iron unit maintains its gleaming good looks for a long time, but is expensive and difficult to install because of its weight. High-gloss acrylic tubs dull over time, but are much easier to work with. Ask a salesperson to show you one in action to make sure you don't get a noisy clunker.

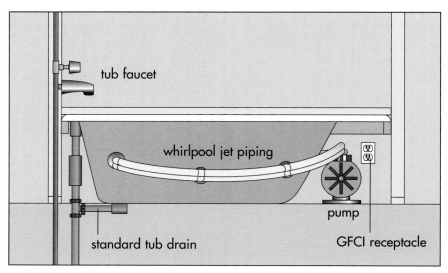

How a whirlpool tub works.
A whirlpool tub must have a removable access panel so you can service the pump and plumbing and electrical connections.

The drain and the water supplies are the same as for a standard tub; it fills with a normal tub faucet. You must use a ground-fault circuit interrupter (GFCI) receptacle operated from a switch on a bathroom wall at least 2 feet from the tub. The receptacle must be on its own circuit. With most units, you simply plug the pump into the outlet.

YOU'LL NEED:

TIME: A day and a half to remove an old tub, prepare the space, and install a new tub. More time may be needed to patch walls and tile.
SKILLS: Plumbing, carpentry, and some wiring.
TOOLS: Hammer and pry bar, pliers, pipe wrench, reciprocating saw or keyhole saw, drill, screwdriver.

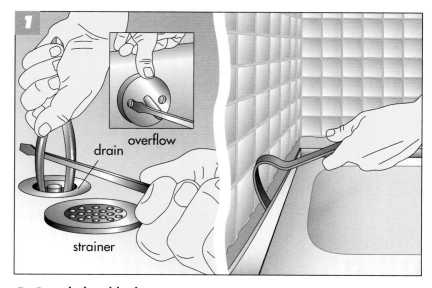

1. Detach the old tub.
Note: *Shut off the water and drain the line.* Loosen the screws on the overflow plate and remove it. Pull out the lever and linkage. Remove the strainer and use pliers and a screwdriver, as shown, to unscrew the drain piece. You may need to pull out a stopper to which linkage pieces are attached.

Chisel away a few tiles, if necessary, and pry the tub loose. You may need to pull nails, unfasten screws, or disconnect clips holding the tub to the wall. Pull the tub away from the wall and remove it.

REMOVING AN OLD TUB

■ Depending on the layout of your bathroom, you might be able to tilt the tub up and carry it out the door. Have at least one helper on hand.

■ In some situations, the only solution is to cut a hole in a wall, without disturbing the plumbing, and slide the tub through into the next room. This is not as drastic as it sounds. You may have to cut only one or two studs, and the wall patching may be less work than you would have with other methods of removal.

■ If the tub is cast iron, by far the easiest way to remove it is to break it apart with a sledgehammer. Wear protective eye wear and work gloves. Remove or cover any items in the bathroom that might be scratched.

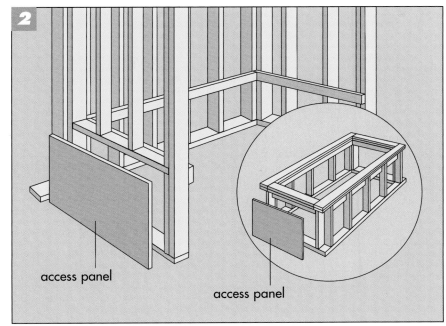

access panel

access panel

2. Prepare the walls.
Check your manufacturer's instructions for framing requirements. In most cases, the tub must rest entirely on the floor—the flange or lip of the tub is not designed to carry the weight of a filled tub. Install pieces of 2×4 to gently support the lip. Be sure to factor in the bed, if any (Step 4), when measuring for these supports. You will run a bead of caulk to fill in the gap after the tub is installed.

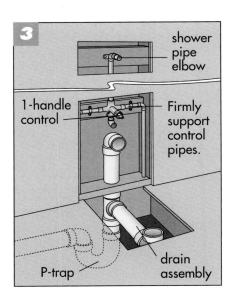

shower pipe elbow

1-handle control

Firmly support control pipes.

P-trap

drain assembly

3. Install the rough plumbing.
Here is a typical installation for a tub. If yours is a new installation, see *Better Homes and Gardens® Step-By-Step Plumbing* for more information on running these lines. Make sure the faucet and shower head (if any) are at the correct height.

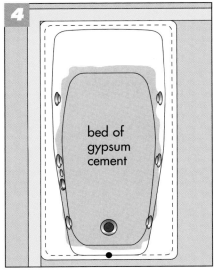

bed of gypsum cement

4. Set the tub in a bed.
If the tub is steel or acrylic, support it well to minimize noise and heat loss. Set the tub in a 2-inch-thick layer of gypsum cement. Or, if noise is not a concern, apply gobs of construction adhesive to the bottom of the tub feet.

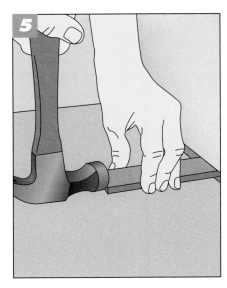

5. Shim and level.
Check the tub for level in both directions and insert shims where needed. Use plenty of construction adhesive to be sure the shims stay in place during years of vibrating whirlpool action.

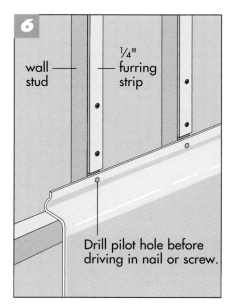

wall stud — ¼" furring strip

Drill pilot hole before driving in nail or screw.

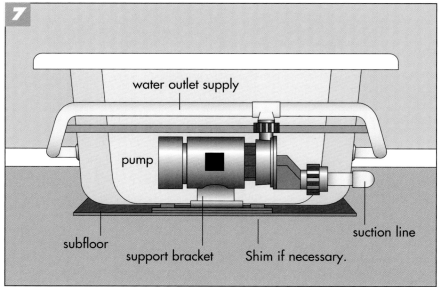

water outlet supply

pump

subfloor

support bracket

Shim if necessary.

suction line

6. Attach flange.

Some tub models have integral flanges designed to be attached directly to wall studs. Drill pilot holes to avoid cracking the tub, and drive nails or screws into each stud. Install ¼-inch-thick furring strips to the studs so the wall material covers up the flange.

7. Anchor the pump.

Cut loose the packing strap and shim the bottom of the pump if necessary to maintain a downward slope on the suction line. Check the line with a level. Do not raise the pump too high—just enough so water can run down through the line. Make sure the pump is not in contact with anything that could cause noise during its operation. Then firmly screw the support bracket to the floor.

CAUTION!
GUARD AGAINST THE EFFECTS OF VIBRATION

■ *No matter how stable the unit is or how well you install it, there will be vibration every time you turn on the whirlpool motor. This means all the connections must be extra tight. Use plenty of Teflon tape or pipe joint compound on the drain fittings and tighten them securely. Also make sure the supply connections are secure.*

■ *Once each year, remove the access panel and check the connections for leaks while the tub is in operation.*

■ *Take extra care when you make the electrical connections. The plug that is inserted into the receptacle will vibrate somewhat, possibly causing wires to come loose from the receptacle if they are not fastened securely.*

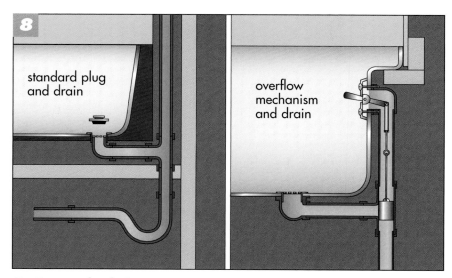

standard plug and drain

overflow mechanism and drain

8. Connect the drain.

For a whirlpool tub, the drain connection is simple. Connect all the pieces and tighten the nuts so the rubber washers seal well. Make the final connection to the bottom of the tub by applying a bead of plumber's putty to the drain piece of the flange, then screwing it on. Hook up the supply lines and install the faucet handles, spigot, and shower head.

For a standard tub, you also need to attach the overflow plate and the overflow mechanism, as shown. Or purchase a pop-up drain mechanism that opens and closes the drain with a push of your toe.

To test for leaks, fill the tub with water, run the motor for a while, and then drain the water, watching carefully with a flashlight all the time.

REFINISHING A TUB

There are plenty of tub refinishers out there, all with fabulous claims about their services. But they may charge nearly as much as it would cost to put in a new tub, and their results are not necessarily a lot better than what you can achieve yourself. Refinishing a tub saves the cost and trouble of a new installation, but the process has its weaknesses. A refinished surface can't withstand bath mats, abrasive cleaners, standing water, or constant drips.

YOU'LL NEED:

TIME: 3 days of several hours work and 3 days of drying time.
SKILLS: Applying automotive body patch, careful painting.
TOOLS: Sanding block, paint brush, putty knives.

WHAT TO DO WHEN YOUR TUB IS DAMAGED

■ Hire a refinisher. For the best results, get someone who uses urethane rather than epoxy or other paint products. Urethane maintains its color well and expands and contracts with changing temperatures to prevent cracks in the finish.

A refinisher should apply at least three coats. You will have to wait three days before using the tub. The test of a refinishing is how long it bears up. Seek out a company that has been around for awhile and likely will be around in the future to back up their work.

■ Purchase a tub insert. Inserts fit exactly into your tub and are glued tightly to it to produce a high-gloss acrylic surface similar to new acrylic tubs. The cost will be more than refinishing.

■ Brush on a finish yourself. This will not be as durable or as smooth as a professional urethane finish. But if you are careful, it can last a long time and will cost a lot less than hiring a professional refinisher.

■ Install a new tub. You may be able to get a new steel or acrylic tub for close to the price of professional refinishing. Keep in mind the drawbacks of these tubs (see page 57).

cover fixtures with masking

1. Prepare the surface.
Carefully remove or mask off the metal parts and the wall tiles. Thoroughly clean the tub and sand it twice, using medium, then fine sandpaper. Fill in chips or indentations with auto body filler and sand smooth. Once you have done this, it is best to wait at least overnight so the tub will be absolutely dry when you paint it. Do not paint during humid weather conditions.

tape edge to protect wall

2. Mix and paint.
The epoxy paint comes in two parts. Thoroughly mix as much as you will need. Use a high-quality brush. The trick is to paint only in one direction and to go over the surface only once. If you try to touch up a spot a minute or so after painting it, the paint will pull away. Apply a second coat the next day. Allow a day of drying time and pull away the masking tape.

ADDING A SHOWER SURROUND

Plastic tub surrounds to accommodate a shower have improved greatly in appearance in recent years. While a bit harder to install than they seem, these units can transform your tub area in only a day.

As you plan the layout of the panels, don't assume the tub is level. Mark a level line on the walls, positioned so when the panel bottom is trimmed to within ⅛ inch of the tub, the top of the panels will be level. If your panels are molded to look like tiles, make sure the seams line up.

YOU'LL NEED:

TIME: 1 day if no major wall repairs are needed.
SKILLS: Measuring, drilling, scribing, and planing.
TOOLS: Tape measure, level, drill, bits, utility knife, block plane, caulking gun, 1× braces.

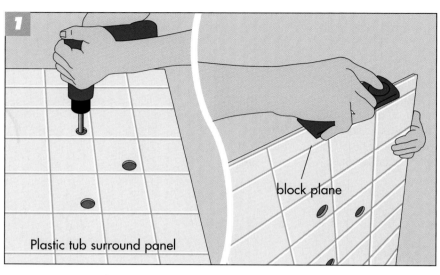

block plane

Plastic tub surround panel

1. Prepare panels.

After making needed repairs to the walls (see page 101), remove the faucet handles and tub spout. Measure the locations of the faucets and spout and mark the panel for boring. Drill each hole ¼ to ½ inch larger than needed to allow for some play when positioning the panels. When boring the holes, lay the panel over a piece of 2×. Scribe and trim the faucet-side panel to fit, then trim the opposite panel. Dry-fit the side panels in place before trimming the back panel.

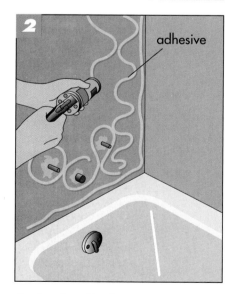

adhesive

2. Apply adhesive.

Check the panel manufacturer's recommendation for adhesive and purchase an adequate amount (typically two cartridges for a three-sided tub enclosure). Encircle the faucet controls and spout pipe with adhesive. Apply the adhesive in a squiggly pattern.

3. Affix the panels.

Set the panels in place and press them firmly into the adhesive. Push hard, making sure the panel completely adheres to the wall. Then pull the panel back off the wall and let the adhesive dry for a minute or two, according to the manufacturer's instructions.

"Spring" these pieces.

4. Brace the panels.

Press the panels back in place. Cut scrap 1×4s and 1×2s to brace the panels while the adhesive sets overnight. Then remove the bracing and seal the panels along the tub edge and in the corners with a mildew-resistant tub-and-tile caulk.

INSTALLING A GLASS SHOWER DOOR

Here's a quick way to make a dramatic difference in the appearance of your bathroom. A glass shower door lets in more light than most shower curtains and does a better job of containing shower spray. The shower door shown is attached to a bathtub that has walls on both ends. Doors are available for shower-only units as well.

Your walls should be square to the tub and parallel with each other. If the walls are off by more than ½ inch, the doors will gap noticeably at the frame.

YOU'LL NEED

TIME: About 2 hours.
SKILLS: Measuring, cutting metal, drilling through tile, caulking.
TOOLS: Tape measure, level, hacksaw, drill, masonry bit, caulking gun, screwdriver.

EXPERTS' INSIGHT

DOOR OR CURTAIN?

For many people, a shower curtain is less expensive and actually preferable to a glass door. However, curtains are more likely to develop mildew, unless you remember to extend the curtain fully after showering so it's not scrunched together. If your bathroom is used a lot and doesn't have a vent fan or time to dry out, a glass door will not guarantee against mildew, but it may cut down on your work. Mildew on a door can be wiped off quickly, while a mildewed curtain has to be taken down, washed in a tub or washing machine, then hung up again.

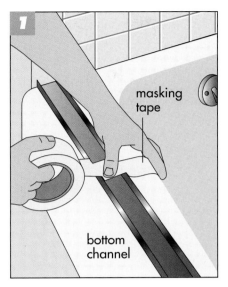

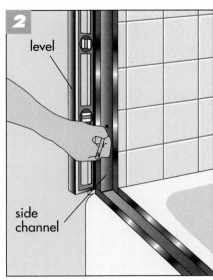

1. Cut and attach bottom channel.
Measure the length of the tub from wall to wall and cut the bottom channel with a hacksaw. Run a substantial bead of silicone caulk along the tub or on the bottom of the channel, position it, and tape it in place while it dries.

2. Install side and top channels.
Plumb each side panel, mark the screw locations, and drill pilot holes. For tile walls, use a masonry bit to drill holes big enough so the screw shanks won't crack the tile. If there is no stud, insert plastic anchors into the wall—not the tile. Screw the channels in place.

3. Add top channel, install door.
Measure and cut the top channel and fit it in place. Apply a bead of silicone caulk along the inside edges of the door frame. No fasteners are required to hold the top channel in place; the weight of the doors does the job. Install the doors by lifting them into place so their rollers fit into the tracks in the top channel. Once the doors are hung, fasten the guides provided with the kit to the bottom of the doors.

INSTALLING A FIBERGLASS SHOWER UNIT

You have plenty of options when it comes to a shower-only installation. Most fiberglass kit installations require three basic tasks: framing any new walls, installing the plumbing, and finishing walls. For plumbing skills, see pages 86–91. If you want to tile the walls, a separate operation, see pages 78–79.

Decide where you want to put the shower. You need a space at least 32 inches square, not including the thickness of any new walls you may have to build. Keep in mind, however, a 36-inch-square unit is much more comfortable and well worth

making room for. Be sure to leave enough room so the shower door can open freely without bumping into a toilet, sink, or vanity.

Next, plan the rough plumbing. Be sure the drain line will be vented adequately (see page 87), and you will not seriously weaken joists when you run the drainpipe. The water supply lines are usually less of a problem—just tap into and extend existing hot and cold lines. If you are not sure about the plumbing, it is a good idea to hire a professional to rough-in the drain and supply lines and to set the shower base.

Sometimes during new house

construction, plumbers install plumbing lines for possible future use. You may be lucky enough to have the drain line you need already poking up through the basement floor.

YOU'LL NEED

TIME: Several days to rough-in the walls and plumbing and to install the shower unit.
SKILLS: Plumbing, carpentry, wall preparation, and tiling.
TOOLS: Complete set of carpentry, drywall taping, plumbing, and tiling tools.

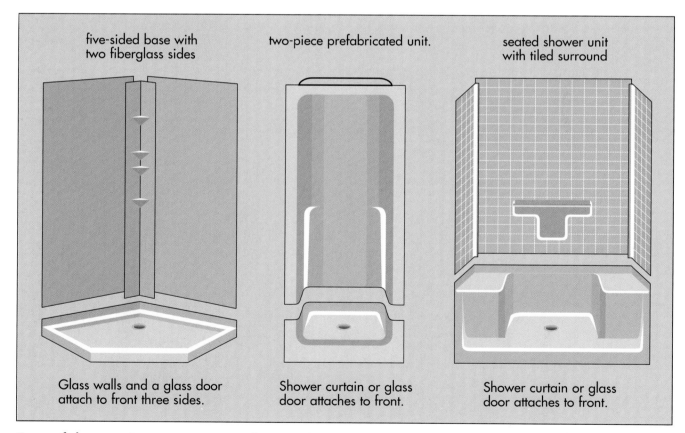

five-sided base with two fiberglass sides

two-piece prefabricated unit.

seated shower unit with tiled surround

Glass walls and a glass door attach to front three sides.

Shower curtain or glass door attaches to front.

Shower curtain or glass door attaches to front.

Types of shower units.
Prefabricated shower stalls usually include the base and complete framing instructions. Before you buy, make sure the pieces will fit through your bathroom door.

Often a multipiece unit will fit where a two-piece unit may not. A corner unit, like the one with the five-sided base, is the easiest to install because it requires no framing. The two-piece unit is the

most common and is ideal when you're able to use an adjacent closet space to add a shower. For the elderly or handicapped, a unit with a seat and assistance bar is a good choice.

PLANNING TIPS FOR SHOWER INSTALLATIONS

Keep these things in mind as you plan your shower:

■ Choose the complete shower ensemble—base, stall, door, faucet, and showerhead—at the same time.

■ Unless you have another source of ventilation, install a bathroom vent fan near the shower. Otherwise, moisture could cause mildew problems.

■ Consider hiring a professional to install the shower base and vented drain. Installing the water supply lines, faucet, and wall panels are easier tasks.

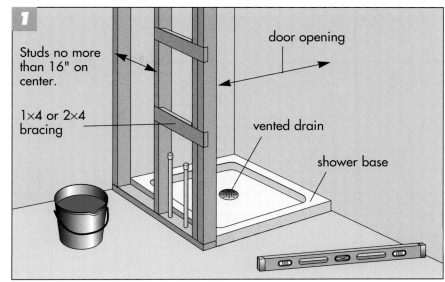

1. Install the base, frame.
Use the dimensions given in the instructions that came with the shower base to install a vented drain in the middle of the shower area. Set the base and hook up the drain. Test for leaks by pouring buckets of water down the drain.

Frame walls that need support, with studs no more than 16 inches on center. Run the framing all the way up to the ceiling or plan on adding a finished ledge to the top of your shower wall(s). Check carefully for plumb and square as you work.

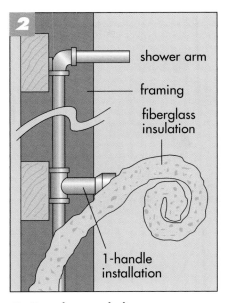

2. Run the supply lines.
Follow the manufacturer's instructions to run the plumbing for the faucet and showerhead. Attach the faucet and the shower arm to the framing with straps or clamps (see page 78). To reduce noise, install insulation between the studs. Slice the insulation's foil or paper face so moisture will not get trapped inside the walls.

3. Install drywall and panels.
Units made of thin material may require installation of greenboard drywall first. Attach the greenboard with construction adhesive and screws. You may need to cut holes in the shower unit for the faucet and shower arm. Attach the panels with adhesive. Run a bead of silicone caulk along all inside joints.

4. Finish the walls.
You may have corners or backs of walls to finish. Apply greenboard drywall and tape the seams. Install metal corner bead at the outside corners. Apply several coats of joint compound over the seams. Then, sand the compound smooth, prime the entire surface, and paint.

BUILDING A TILED SHOWER

As you plan the best location for the shower, leave enough room so it's easy to use. If vented drain and water supply lines do not exist, you will need to install them. Unless you have plumbing experience you may want to have a professional handle this job.

Don't place the shower in a corner of the bathroom just to save work; framing new walls is a fairly small part of this job. Starting with plumb, square walls makes it much easier to achieve a professional-looking job. If space allows, frame the shower completely, as shown in Step 2, to be sure the walls will be plumb and square.

Plan the tiling carefully. Purchase bullnose pieces (caps) for every place where the edge of a tile will be visible, as well as corner pieces where two edges will be visible. Decide exactly where

you want the tiles to stop. For instance, you may want to wrap tile around the thickness of the walls where the door will be.

It's usual to put in a glass door for a unit like this. However, a curtain may be a good choice if you have limited space.

YOU'LL NEED

TIME: 3 or 4 days to install plumbing; frame, tile, and grout the inside; and finish the outside wall(s).
SKILLS: Framing, plumbing, taping, and tiling skills.
TOOLS: Tubing cutter or hacksaw, emory cloth, wire brush, flux brush, propane torch, pliers, wrenches, bucket, level, hammer, tape measure, taping knife, knife or keyhole saw, plumb bob, notched trowel, drill with masonry bit, screwdriver.

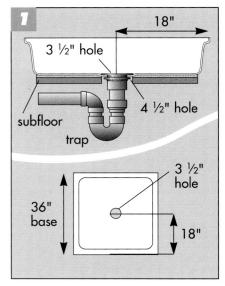

1. Install a base with drain.
Run a properly vented drain line to the center of the shower base (pad). Install the base and connect the drain. Test for leaks by pouring buckets of water down the drain.

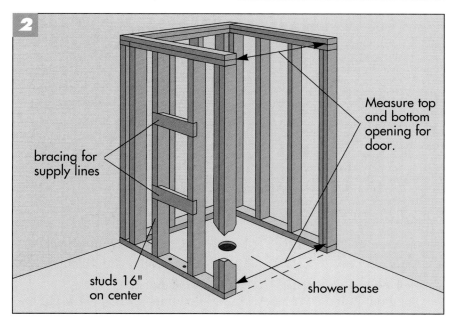

2. Frame the enclosure.
Decide whether you want walls up to the ceiling or a ledge about 7 feet high. As you plan the framing, include the correct size of opening for the door, factoring in the thickness of the tiles; room for running the supply lines exactly

where you want them; studs placed no more than 16 inches on center; nailing surfaces for all pieces of greenboard or cement board; and bracing for the supply lines. Check carefully that everything is square and plumb.

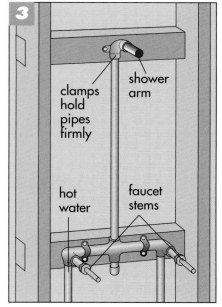

3. Run the supplies.
Note: *Be sure to shut off the water.* Tap into hot and cold water lines and run new lines to the shower (see pages 86–91). Install the faucets as per manufacturer's directions. Anchor the supply pipes firmly to the bracing boards.

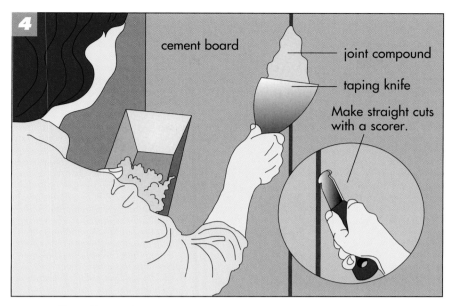

cement board

joint compound

taping knife

Make straight cuts with a scorer.

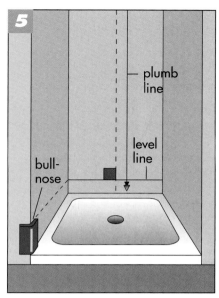

plumb line

level line

bull-nose

4. Install wall covering, tape.

Cut and fit pieces of cement board for the inside of the enclosure and greenboard drywall for any walls on the outside (see pages 102–103). Use a cement-board scorer (or, in a pinch, a utility knife) for straight cuts and a keyhole saw to cut holes for pipes.

Install corner bead on the outside corners. Cover the joints with joint compound. For outside walls that will be painted, apply joint tape and three or more coats of joint compound, and sand smooth. Areas to be tiled do not need to be as smooth as those to be painted, but should not have bumps.

5. Lay out for the tiles.

Carefully establish horizontal and vertical layout lines. Make sure you will not end up with small slivers of tiles in corners and avoid having different-sized tiles on either side of a wall. Make sure bullnose pieces will end up placed on the edges.

notched trowel

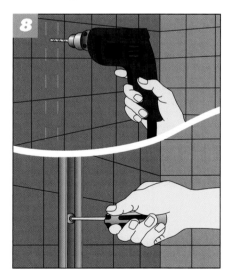

6. Lay the tiles.

Spread tile adhesive with a trowel with the correct size of notches. Try not to obscure your guide lines. Apply adhesive to a small area, then begin setting tiles. Give each tile a little twist and push to make sure it sticks. Wipe away excess adhesive immediately. Allow the tiles to set at least a day, then grout (see page 41).

7. Install the finish plumbing.

After the grout has dried, slide on the flanges and hook up the faucet handle(s) and showerhead. Make sure the area around the faucet is well sealed; if your unit does not have a rubber gasket that seats tightly against the wall, apply a bead of silicone caulk.

8. Install the door.

For a sliding glass door, cut the bottom and top channels and install them. Hold each side channel so it is plumb and parallel to the tile lines and mark for the holes. Drill through the tiles carefully with a masonry bit, apply silicone caulk to the wall or back of the channel, and drive in screws to attach the channel. Apply a bead of caulk around all channels.

REPLACING A TOILET

Replacing a toilet is not complicated. Often, however, doing so reveals rotted flooring that must be repaired before the toilet is set back in place. If you uncover water damage, you'll have to remove the damaged flooring and patch it.

Work carefully to avoid cracking the toilet. Most toilets sold today have drains centered 12 inches from the back wall. To find the drain location, measure from the wall to the hold-down bolt on the toilet. If it is centered 10 inches from the wall, either buy a 10-inch toilet or install a special offset closet flange. If the toilet water supply line does not have a stop valve, install one (see page 91).

YOU'LL NEED

TIME: About 3 hours to remove an old toilet and install a new one; several hours more if the floor needs repairs.
SKILLS: Basic plumbing skills.
TOOLS: Adjustable wrench, screwdriver, hacksaw, tongue-and-groove pliers, putty knife, reciprocating or circular saw, drill.

TIME SAVER

IF THE FLANGE IS LOW

If your bathroom has a new layer of flooring, the closet flange often ends up below the floor surface. In that case, a regular wax ring may not be thick enough to seal the toilet bowl to the flange. Rather than changing the plumbing, you can extend the ring upward with a flange extender or add a second wax ring to make up the difference.

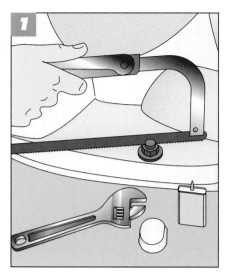

1. Remove the old toilet.
Note: *Shut off the water.* Flush the toilet and sponge out water left in the tank. Disconnect the supply line and unscrew the hold-down nuts. If these are rusted tight, try penetrating oil or cut off the nuts with a hacksaw.

Cut right up to the joists.

2. Cut out damaged flooring.
If the floor is rotted, lift up the flooring surface and explore with a hammer and screwdriver to find out how far the damage extends. Using a reciprocating saw or circular saw, cut out a rectangular hole up to the joists on either side.

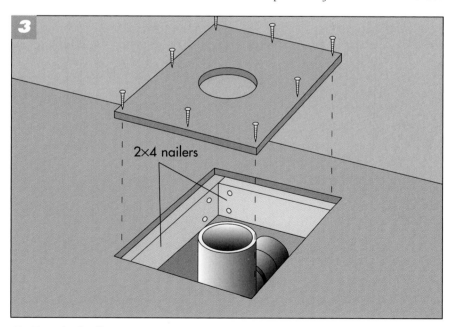

2×4 nailers

3. Repair the floor.
Mount 2×4s to the joists to provide a nailing surface for the floor patch. Cut the nailers for the joists a bit long and hold them so their top edges are tight to the bottom of the flooring as you drive in screws to attach them to the joists. Cut the cross pieces to fit snugly and attach them with angle-driven screws. When you install your patch, you may need to shim it up to get it exactly flush with the rest of the floor. Cut the piece and install it with screws.

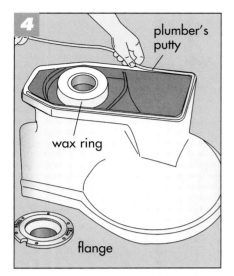

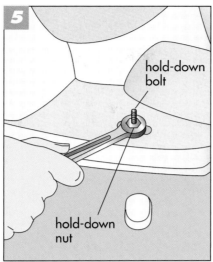

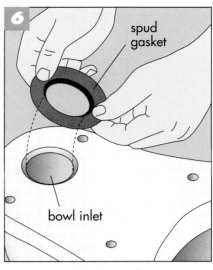

4. Prepare the new toilet bowl.

Carefully remove the bowl from its box and turn it upside down on a cushioned surface, such as a drop cloth or bath mat. Run a rope of plumber's putty around the perimeter of the base and fit a wax ring (sold separately) over the outlet opening. For a cast-iron flange, it is best to place the wax ring on the flange rather than on the toilet.

5. Attach the bowl.

Turn the bowl upright and set it in place on top of the closet flange. Make sure the hold-down bolts align with the holes in the base. Press down on the bowl with both hands; turn it so it looks straight. Slip a metal washer and a nut over each bolt and slowly tighten one bolt a bit, then the other. Stop when the bowl sits flat on the floor and feels solid.

6. Prepare for the tank.

Lay the spud gasket, beveled side down, over the bowl inlet opening. Or slip the spud gasket onto the threaded tailpiece located at the bottom of the tank. This forms the seal between the tank and the bowl.

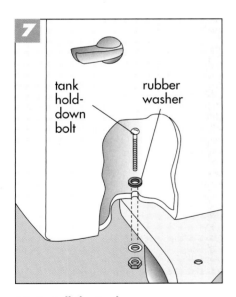

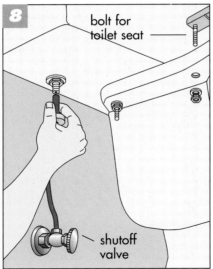

7. Install the tank.

Gently lower the tank onto the bowl, aligning the tank holes with those toward the rear of the bowl. Secure the tank to the bowl with the hold-down bolts, washers, and nuts provided with the toilet. Be sure the rubber washer gets under the bolt head inside the tank.

8. Attach the water supply.

The easiest hook-up for a water supply line is a flexible plastic or chrome-braided supply line. Tighten both ends by hand, then give the nuts half a turn or so with pliers. Or use chrome-finished flexible copper tubing and compression fittings (see page 90).

EXPERTS' INSIGHT

WATER-SAVING TOILETS

Most local plumbing codes require new toilets to use only 1.6 gallons of water per flush. These save money by reducing water consumption. They differ from older models only by having a smaller tank or a mechanism that restricts the amount of water in the tank. Don't buy a new toilet simply to save money in water usage. Reduce an old toilet's consumption by setting a brick or filled half-gallon plastic bottle into the tank or by bending the float ball rod downward.

Most newer toilet models have reduced flushing power. If this is a problem for you, purchase a pressure-assisted toilet.

INSTALLING A MEDICINE CABINET

Nothing quite stores toiletries as close to the point of use and as nicely out of sight as a medicine cabinet. Most cabinets are positioned for adult use; find a placement that suits the various heights in your household.

Getting the lighting right can be difficult. Most cabinets that come with lighting kits have the lights positioned above the mirror, even though sidelights tend to provide better illumination. If the lighting in your bathroom is more than adequate, for example, multiple recessed fixtures, you likely can get by with a simple cabinet with no lights. If you don't have a nearby outlet, look for a unit with a ground-fault circuit interrupter (GFCI) receptacle.

A flush-mounted cabinet is the easiest to install (see above, right). But it sticks out from the wall, detracting from the visual appearance of the wall. A recessed cabinet is more appealing to the eye, but requires more work. You must cut an opening, and perhaps notch a stud, before it will slide in. But it is worth the extra work if you need the space.

If your bathroom does not have a recessed cabinet, it may be because there are pipes or electrical cables in the wall. You may be able to buy a flush-mounted unit and recess it partially, as shown on page 83.

YOU'LL NEED

TIME: 1 to 2 hours for a simple unit; most of a day if you need to do electrical wiring.
SKILLS: Carpentry and electrical skills.
TOOLS: Utility knife, keyhole or reciprocating saw, drill, level, hammer. For electrical connections, a wire stripper, lineman's pliers, needle-nosed pliers, screwdriver.

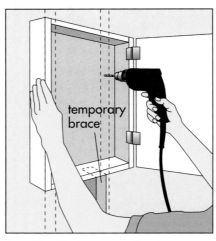

Install a flush-mounted unit.
Purchase a unit with finished sides designed to be flush-mounted. Locate the wall studs by tapping a nail through the wall in places that will get covered up by the cabinet. Open the cabinet door and temporarily brace the cabinet so it is plumb and centered over the sink. Drive screws through the cabinet and into studs.

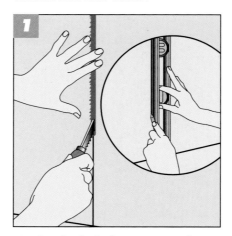

1. Cut the hole for a recessed unit.
Draw an outline of your cabinet on the wall, centered above the sink at a good height for as many members of your family as possible. Plumb the markings for level placement. Score the outline first with a knife and level, then cut it out with a keyhole or reciprocating saw. Remove the drywall or plaster and lath. If there is a stud in the way, notch it to accommodate your cabinet.

CAUTION!
TAKE CARE BEFORE CUTTING INTO WALLS
Don't just mark a wall and start cutting with a reciprocating or keyhole saw. You may puncture a pipe or sever an electrical cable. If you have the blueprints for your house, they may show you the location of pipes and wires. In any case, cut carefully and slowly, feeling for differences in your saw's behavior. To be extra safe, cut a small opening first and check for obstructions with a flashlight and a stick before making your final hole. If you find pipes or wiring, it's easier to install a flush-mounted unit rather than redoing plumbing or electrical connections.

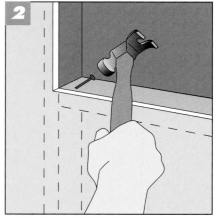

2. Frame the opening.
You may or may not have vertical studs to attach the cabinet to. You don't have to frame all around the opening for the medicine cabinet, but you should firmly attach pieces of 2× at the top and bottom to secure it. Cut them to fit snugly and toenail or screw them to the studs. Reanchor the drywall or plaster to the edge of the studs with screws.

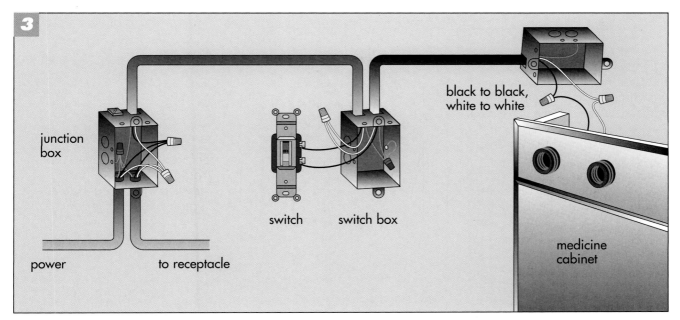

junction box

power

to receptacle

switch

switch box

black to black, white to white

medicine cabinet

3. Wire for a light, receptacle.
Note: *Shut off power.* Run cable to the opening. For a light only, run the power directly to the switch and then to the cabinet. To wire a receptacle and a light, as shown above, run power to a junction box, then branch it to the receptacle and switch. If you need both a receptacle and a light, wire as shown for a receptacle that is always hot. Provide grounding, either with a ground wire or by means of metal sheathing. (See pages 92–99 for wiring basics.) Strip the cable sheathing and about ¾ inch of insulation from each wire. For each connection, twist the wires together with lineman's pliers, screw on a wire connector, and wrap with electrical tape. Connect the ground wire to the screw provided. Close the cover, restore power, and test.

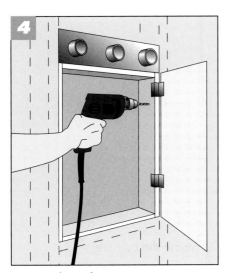

4. Set the cabinet.
Once the electrical cable is attached to the cabinet, slide the cabinet into place. Check that it is plumb and centered on the sink and sets flush to the wall. Install one of the upper screws and check for plumb again. Then attach it to the framing pieces by driving in the rest of the screws.

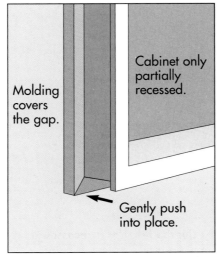

Molding covers the gap.

Cabinet only partially recessed.

Gently push into place.

Trim a partially recessed cabinet.
If you were not able to slide the cabinet all the way flush to the wall because plumbing or wiring was in the way, insert the cabinet so it sticks out of the wall the same distance at all points. Wrap it with molding to cover the gap between the cabinet and the wall. Small-width door casing is a good choice for this molding.

EXPERTS' INSIGHT

INSTALLING A TOGGLE SWITCH ON THE MEDICINE CABINET

If local electrical codes allow, you can install a small toggle switch on the cabinet itself. This saves you the trouble of hacking into walls to fish cable and install a standard switch. Do this only if there is room on the face or side of the cabinet for the switch and if there is a cavity available so the cable will not be exposed. Be sure to ground the light—you'll have to attach the ground wire some place other than near the switch.

ADDING A MIRROR WITH LIGHTS

If you don't need the cabinet storage space, a large mirror over the sink adds the illusion of space in a bathroom. Hanging the mirror requires no special skills, but you must work carefully and have a sure-handed helper on hand. Glass companies may install the mirror for you for a reasonable price.

YOU'LL NEED

TIME: Once the electrical box is in place, about 1 hour to install the mirror.
SKILLS: Basic electrical skills, careful measuring and careful handling of a large piece of glass.
TOOLS: Keyhole saw, drill, electrical tools.

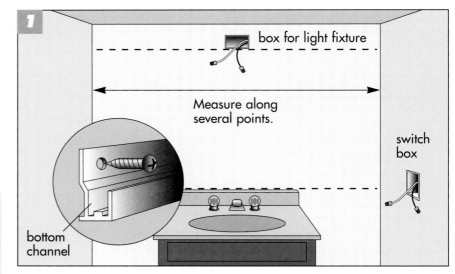

1. Order glass, install channel.
If your mirror extends from wall to wall, check carefully for square, measuring at several points along the way. Give the glass dealer the exact measurements of the space, and ask them to subtract the correct amount to take into account trim pieces. Usually, the trim allows ⅜ inch or so of wiggle room. To bear the weight of the mirror, make sure to install the bottom channel by driving screws into wall studs.

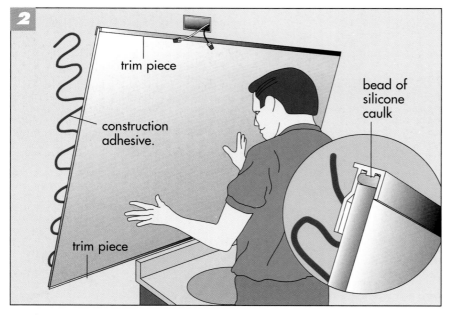

2. Install the mirror.
This method works for most situations. Dry-fit the mirror with the trim pieces in place to make sure there is sufficient room. Take the mirror down and apply squiggles of construction adhesive to the wall. Run a bead of silicone caulk inside the top and side trim pieces—enough so the trim adheres to the mirror. Slip the trim on the mirror and set the mirror in place. (You may need a helper with a large mirror.) Adjust the trim as needed. Hold the mirror in place until the adhesive sets. If possible, brace it in place as shown on page 74.

3. Install the light fixture.
Wire the light, connecting the ground wire as well as the black and white wires. Hook up the switch, restore power, and test the light. See pages 98–99 for ways to connect lights to an electrical box.

ADDING BATH ACCESSORIES

Sometimes a bathroom can be brightened significantly by removing the old hardware, painting the walls, and installing new accessories. Select a group of amenities that go well together. Don't be shy about buying more expensive hardware; the price is relatively small in comparison to most improvements.

Place towel racks where towels can hang about two-thirds of their full length. You probably will not be able to position the rack so the screws hit wall studs, but you do want some strength. Use toggle bolts rather than plastic wall anchors, which are not as strong. If you have lath-and-plaster walls, screwing into a piece of lath may provide adequate support. If you lack sufficient wall space, a rack or hook on the back of the door comes in handy.

One attractive type of soap dish installs right into a tiled wall. Remove two tiles, apply adhesive, then tape the dish in place until the adhesive sets. Finish the edges with caulk or grout. To install a standard recessed toilet-paper holder, drill test holes to make sure you will not run into a stud. Cut the hole carefully so you won't have to patch the wall. Use construction adhesive and (if possible) screws to anchor a piece of 2×4 to the back of the cavity. Let the adhesive dry and attach the holder to the 2×4 with screws.

A secure handgrip is a helpful aid for the elderly or disabled. For security, you must locate the wall studs and drive screws into them.

YOU'LL NEED

TIME: 1 to 2 hours for most installations.
SKILLS: Measuring, leveling, drilling, using toggle bolts.
TOOLS: Tape measure, level, drill, screwdriver, caulking gun.

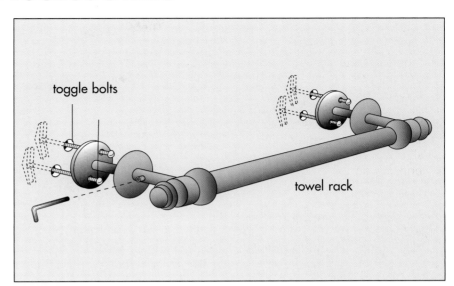
toggle bolts
towel rack

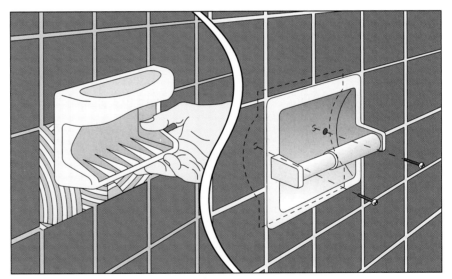

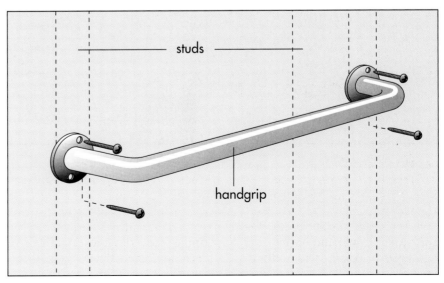
studs
handgrip

PLUMBING

All those crisscrossing pipes in your house can seem complicated and mysterious. But the basic job of your plumbing system is simple: distributing incoming water to where it's wanted and providing a safe path for wastewater to leave the house.

Locate your water meter and main shutoff valves.

Before you do plumbing work in your house, be sure to locate the water meter and, more importantly, the main shutoff valve in the house. In fact, every homeowner should know how to shut off the water to the house to minimize damage from a burst pipe or other plumbing emergency.

You may have a main shutoff outside the house, buried in a cavity often called a "buffalo box." Here you may find a valve with a handle you can turn by hand. If you find you need a special tool to turn it off, be sure to keep one of

these "keys" (usually with long handles) readily available.

Next, look for the place where water enters your house. Usually, you'll find a pipe about an inch thick, called a water main, coming through the floor or wall of your basement or first floor. If you have metered water, the pipe will enter and exit a water meter, a metal unit with either a digital readout or a series of dials. There will be shutoff valves on both sides of the meter. If you have a well or if your bill does not change no matter how much water you use, you won't have a water meter.

Know where your responsibility begins and ends.

Most homes have a water meter. This is an important boundary. The meter and the pipes leading to it are the responsibility of the water company; everything on the house side is your responsibility. If you will be adding new fixtures

THE OLD AND THE NEW

■ An old house may have cast-iron drain lines, which are fitted together with molten lead, and galvanized pipe, which is strong but will rust and corrode over time. Modern plastic drain lines and copper supply lines are superior to the old materials. They're easier to work with and last longer.

■ If you have old pipes, there's no need to rip them out. Many products now are available that make it easy to connect the new to the old. These products often use rubber gaskets that remain leakproof for many decades if installed correctly.

(not just replacing old ones), the local plumbing code may require a larger water main pipe coming into the house. Check when you get a permit.

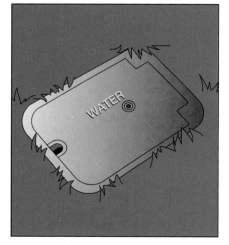

Find your outdoor shutoff.
To find a shutoff outside the house, look for a rectangular plastic lid or a round metal cover in the ground near the street or at the edge of your property. Pry up the cover to find the valve inside. You may need a special key to turn the valve.

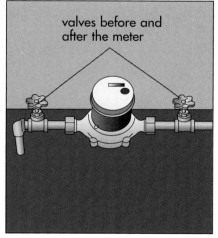

Locate your indoor shutoff.
The shutoff valve in the house usually is located near the water meter. There are usually two valves, one before and one after the meter. Always shut off the one before the meter first to make sure the water pressure does not damage the water meter.

Supply system delivers water.

After entering your house, water generally is routed to a water heater. Then a pair of pipes—one hot and one cold—branch out through the house to serve the various fixtures.

Modern homes have stop (or shutoff) valves just prior to each fixture or appliance. If there are no stop valves next to your fixtures, do yourself a favor and install them. They'll make repairs and emergency shutoffs much easier and more convenient.

Water supply lines are always under pressure. If they are opened or a break occurs, water shoots out and will not stop until it is shut off in some way.

Always shut off the water, either to the whole house or to the specific fixture you are working on, before working on cold or hot water supply pipes.

Drain system carries away waste.

Drains use gravity to rid the house of liquid and solid waste. All fixtures have a trap—a curved section of pipe that holds enough water to make an airtight seal between the fixture and the drain line. Traps guard against foul-smelling and dangerous gases.

Wastewater leaves the traps and moves in pipes sloped downward toward a waste stack, also called a soil pipe. A waste stack is a large, vertical pipe that carries water below the floor. From there, the wastewater flows to a sewer line or a private septic system.

Because drainpipes sometimes become clogged, it is helpful to have cleanouts located at various places along the lines. At a clean-out, you simply unscrew a plug and insert an auger to get at whatever is plugging the drain.

Vent system serves two purposes.

To flow freely, drainpipes need air. Without air, water glugs down a drain like soda pop from a bottle. A plumbing vent plays the same

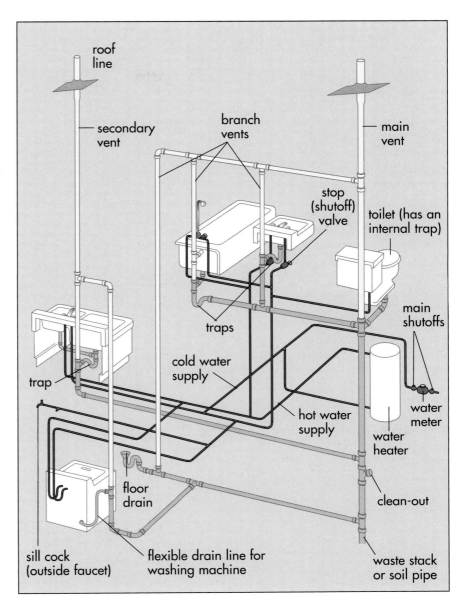

role as that little second opening in a gasoline can; once the stopper is opened, liquid can flow freely. The whole system is often referred to as the drain-waste-vent system, or DWV.

Air supplied by a vent also prevents siphoning action, which might otherwise pull water up and out of traps and toilets. This would allow dangerous sewage gases to escape into the house.

A main vent is an extension of the waste stack and reaches upward through the roof. Branch vents tie into the main vent. Every plumbing fixture and appliance must be vented properly, either by

tying into a main vent or by having a vent of its own that extends through the roof.

When installing a plumbing fixture in a new location (not just replacing an existing fixture), venting is usually the most difficult problem to overcome. You have to run branch vents to an existing main vent or install an additional main vent.

Research your local plumbing and building codes before you start a project. Don't hesitate to call in a professional plumber if you are not sure you are venting the plumbing system properly.

UNDERSTANDING PIPES AND FITTINGS

Water supply pipes usually are made of galvanized steel or copper. Plastic supplies are not allowed by most local building codes; others specify chlorinated polyvinyl chloride (CPVC). New drain lines are almost all plastic, either polyvinyl chloride (PVC) or acrylonitrile butadiene styrene (ABS); these can be added onto cast-iron drains.

Natural gas lines are almost always made of black steel pipe and are installed in the same way as galvanized steel pipe (see page 91). It's important to check for leaks in these pipes. To do so, pour soapy water on the fitting and look for tiny bubbles escaping around the joint.

Before you buy pipe, check with your local building department to make sure you are using material approved for use in your area.

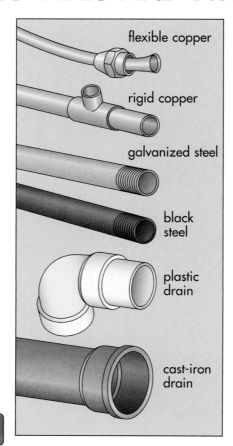

flexible copper
rigid copper
galvanized steel
black steel
plastic drain
cast-iron drain

MEASUREMENTS

SIZING PIPES UP

It is important to buy the correct size of pipe. Pipes are sized according to inside diameter. To measure a pipe from the outside, wrap a piece of string around it and measure the length of the string. To figure the inside diameter for copper pipe, subtract ⅛ inch; for galvanized and cast-iron pipe, subtract ¼ inch; and for plastic pipe, subtract ⅜ inch.
Here are the most common sizes for residential pipes:
■ Main water line: ¾ or 1 inch.
■ Water supply lines: ½ or (less commonly) ¾ inch.
■ Main stacks: 3 or 4 inches.
■ Kitchen sinks and tub, and shower drains: 1½ inches.
■ Bathroom sinks: 1¼ inches.

copper T
copper coupling
galvanized steel supply street L
steel union
steel nipple
plastic-to-copper transition fitting
galvanized-to-copper dielectric transition fitting

Choosing pipe and fittings

It's often easiest to add on pipe of the same type already used in your kitchen or bath. But you can buy transition fittings to switch from one material to another.

Most fittings are available in all materials and all sizes. Use an L fitting (elbow) to make a 90- or 45-degree turn. Most have female threads or openings on each end. A street L has male and female connections for use in tight spots. Use T fittings wherever two runs intersect. Couplings connect pipes end to end. Reducing Ts or reducing couplings allow you to make a transition from one pipe size to another. Use a cap to seal off a line.

Use transition fittings when changing between materials. Be sure to use a dielectric fitting when changing from galvanized steel to copper, or the joint will corrode because of the chemical reaction between the two metals. In any run of threaded pipe, you'll need a union somewhere to compensate for the fact that you can't simultaneously thread a pipe into fittings at either end. Nipples are lengths of pipe less than 12 inches long used to connect fittings or sections of pipe together.

Drainage fittings, also called sanitary fittings, have gentle curves so waste does not get hung up in the pipe. Choose one-quarter bends to make 90-degree turns and one-eighth bends for 45 degrees; other angles also are available. A sanitary T has one curved part for easier drainage. To hook up a toilet, get a closet bend, which connects to the main drain, and a closet flange, which fits onto the bend and is anchored to the floor. Make a transition from cast-iron to plastic pipe with a no-hub adapter or a saddle T, both of which use rubber gaskets to ensure a tight seal.

WORKING WITH RIGID COPPER PIPE

To join rigid copper plumbing lines, you must learn a skill unlike other household remodeling skills—sweat soldering. At first, it will be slow work. But once you get the knack of it, it can be faster than screwing together threaded galvanized pipe. Sweating pipes uses capillary action to flow molten solder into the fitting. Like a blotter soaking up ink, the joint absorbs the solder to make a watertight bond as strong as the pipe itself.

YOU'LL NEED

TIME: With practice, an hour to connect five joints.
SKILLS: Soldering is a specialized skill that takes time to learn.
TOOLS: Tubing cutter or hacksaw, emery cloth, wire brush, flux brush, propane torch, pliers.

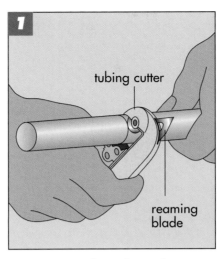

1. Cut pipe, clean the ends.
A tubing cutter makes cleaner and faster cuts. But a hacksaw will do the job; use a miter box for straight cuts. Use the reaming blade of the cutter or a file to remove the burrs on the inside of the pipe. Polish the outside of the pipe and the inside of the fitting with emery cloth.

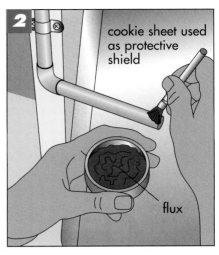

2. Apply flux.
Brush on a light, even coating of flux (also called soldering paste) to both surfaces. Flux retards oxidation when the copper is heated, making the solder adhere better. It will burn away as the solder flows into the joint. Use rosin-type flux. Protect flammable surfaces with a metal shield.

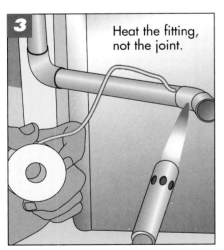

3. Sweat in the connection.
Bend a length of lead-free solder to a usable shape. Fit the pieces together, light the torch, and adjust it so the blue inner flame is about 2 inches long. Heat the middle of the fitting—not the joint. Once the joint is hot, touch the solder to it. If the heat is right, solder will flow into the joint. Remove the flame when the whole joint is filled and solder drips out.

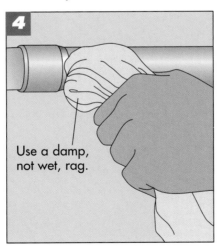

4. Wipe away excess.
Right away, lightly brush the joint with a damp—not wet—rag. Most professionals lay out an entire run of copper, first cutting and dry-fitting all the components. Then they clean, flux, and solder each joint. Check for gaps at the joint. If there are any, the pipe will leak. If the pipe leaks, you'll have to turn off the water, drain the pipe, disassemble it, and sweat it again.

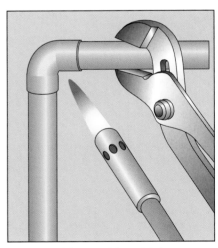

Disassemble a soldered joint.
Note: *Shut off the water.* Never heat a pipe full of water. Drain the line by opening faucets above and below the line. Light the torch and set it so the inner blue core is about 2 inches long. Heat the fitting, pointing the flame at both sides but not at the joint. While it is hot, grasp the fitting and the pipe with tongue-and-groove pliers and pull them apart.

WORKING WITH COMPRESSION FITTINGS

*U*se compression fittings in places where you may need to take the run apart someday or where it is difficult to solder. They are used most often for supply lines for dishwashers and other appliances. Use compression fittings only in accessible places; never bury one in a wall.

Compression fittings are used with flexible copper tubing. Cut the tubing with a tubing cutter and polish its ends as you would rigid copper pipe (page 89). Bend it carefully; once kinked, it is ruined. Use a coil-spring tubing bender to ensure against kinking.

YOU'LL NEED

TIME: About 15 minutes per connection.
SKILLS: No special skills needed.
TOOLS: Two wrenches.

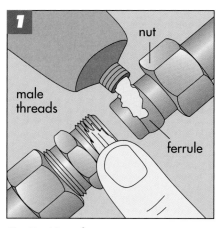

1. Position the parts.
Slip a nut and a ferrule onto each piece of tubing. Smear pipe joint compound on the ferrules and on the male threads of the fitting. Slide the pieces together and hand-tighten the nuts.

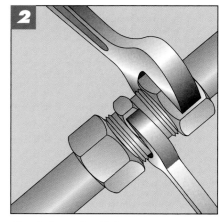

2. Tighten the fitting.
Always use two wrenches or a wrench and a pair of tongue-and-groove pliers. To avoid bending the pipe, hold one nut firmly while you tighten the other. After the nuts are snug, tighten about one-half turn more. Turn on the water and, if there is a leak, gently tighten the fittings further.

WORKING WITH RIGID PLASTIC PIPE

*C*heck local plumbing codes to be sure you are using the correct type of plastic pipe: usually ABS or PVC for drain lines and CPVC for supply lines. Do not connect ABS plastic pipe to PVC pipe. Cut the pipes with a fine-toothed saw and remove all burrs. Assemble plastic pipe carefully; dry-fit several pieces ahead before gluing. Make alignment marks where you make a turn (see Step 2). Once they're glued, you cannot take the pieces apart.

YOU'LL NEED

TIME: With practice, about an hour for five joints.
SKILLS: Careful measuring and cutting, thinking ahead.
TOOLS: Fine-toothed saw, miter box, tape measure, utility knife, emery cloth.

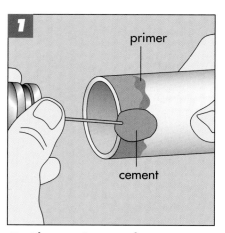

1. Clean, prime, apply cement.
Once you have dry-fit the pieces and made alignment marks, take them apart and set them in order. Work quickly for each joint—the cement sets up rapidly. Check codes to see which primer and cement you should use. Clean the ends of the pipe and fitting and coat with primer. Apply cement to the outside end of the pipe and the inside of the fitting socket.

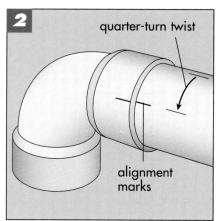

2. Twist and hold.
Push the pieces together, making sure the pipe goes all the way into the socket. Twist it a quarter turn as you push to help spread the cement evenly. Complete the twist until your alignment marks come together. Hold the pipe and fitting together for about 20 seconds while they fuse. Wipe away excess cement with a cloth.

WORKING WITH THREADED PIPE

*U*nless you have access to pipe cutters and threaders, you can't just cut a piece of galvanized steel pipe to fit, as with copper or plastic pipe. So you must plan carefully. The challenge with threaded pipe is ending up at the right place. Purchase long pieces to make up most of the run and have on hand plenty of couplings and a selection of nipples. You will then have a number of options for ending up at the right spot. Often a union comes in handy. With it, you can join pipes at either end.

YOU'LL NEED

TIME: About 1 hour for four pipe lengths with fittings.
SKILLS: Measuring, planning ahead, basic plumbing skills.
TOOLS: Tape measure, two adjustable and/or pipe wrenches.

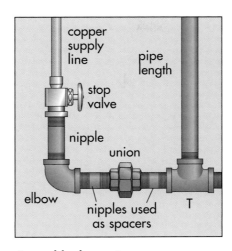

Assemble the parts

Pipe threads screw in only one direction—clockwise—so usually you have to start at one end and proceed in only one direction. To break into a line to add another branch, cut a pipe and remove both ends. Install a combination of smaller pieces: a T for the new branch, nipples, and a union to join it all together.

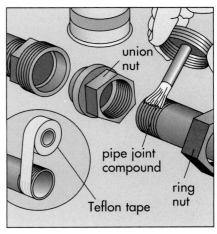

Join the pieces

Before you thread a pipe and fitting together, apply pipe joint compound or Teflon tape to the threads to help seal the joint. Assemble the pieces one at a time, tightening as you go. Use a pipe wrench to ensure the joints are tight. If your assembly requires a union, work from each end toward the union.

INSTALLING STOP VALVES

*S*top valves make it easy to repair faucets and appliances. Without one, any time you need to repair a faucet, dishwasher, or toilet, you have to shut off the water supply to the entire house. They also are handy when you have to shut off a fixture in an emergency. When you purchase a stop valve, be sure the valve's inlet matches your pipe—1/2-inch copper or threaded, in most cases. Choose 1/2- or 3/8-inch outlets and make sure your flexible copper or plastic supply line is the same size.

YOU'LL NEED

TIME: 1 to 2 hours.
SKILLS: Cutting, connecting pipe.
TOOLS: Hacksaw, tongue-and-groove pliers, tubing cutter, adjustable wrench, propane torch (for copper).

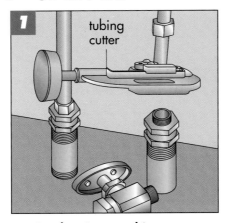

1. Cut the pipe or tubing.

Note: *Shut off the water.* If you have threaded galvanized pipes and a flexible supply line, simply unscrew the supply. For rigid copper or flexible copper tubing, as shown, cut enough off the existing pipe to make room for the valve. Leave enough supply line to allow for tightening the stop valve on the pipe.

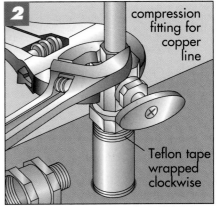

2. Hook up the valve.

For galvanized pipe, as shown, screw on the stop valve. For copper pipe, purchase a unit with a compression inlet and attach it like any compression fitting (see page 90), or get one designed to be soldered on (see page 89). Slip the copper line onto the other end and tighten the fitting. Or screw on a flexible braided supply line.

WIRING

*E*lectricity always flows in a loop, known as a circuit. When a circuit is interrupted, as when a switch is turned off or a wire is disconnected, the electrical current stops. As soon as the circuit is reconnected, as when a switch is turned on, the flow begins again.

Follow the flow.

Electricity from your local electric utility company passes through an electric meter, which measures how much enters your house and proceeds to a main service panel (right), also called a breaker box or a fuse box. There it is broken up into various circuits, each serving a different part of the house. The current flows out of the service panel on "hot" wires with black or colored insulation and returns to the panel on neutral wires with white insulation.

A typical household service begins with three wires to the house: two 120-volt hot lines and a single neutral line. If you have an old house with only two wires coming in, call a professional to get it updated. The service panel contains circuit breakers or fuses, which are safety devices that shut off the power in case of a short circuit or other fault. A single hot and neutral wire combine to form a 120-volt circuit; two hots plus a neutral form a 240-volt circuit for a major appliance.

Always shut off power at the main service panel before working on the wiring in your house.

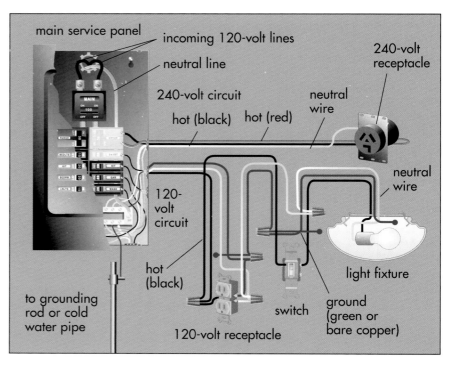

main service panel · incoming 120-volt lines · neutral line · 240-volt receptacle · 240-volt circuit · hot (black) · hot (red) · neutral wire · neutral wire · 120-volt circuit · hot (black) · 120-volt receptacle · switch · light fixture · ground (green or bare copper) · to grounding rod or cold water pipe

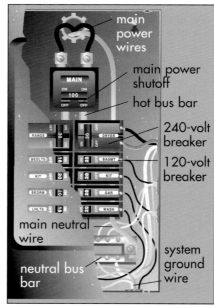

Know your breaker box.

Entering power goes right to the main breaker; turn this off and you cut power to the rest of the box. The main hot wires each energize a hot bus bar. Individual hot wires are connected to the breakers, which are attached to hot bus bars. When a circuit is overloaded or a short occurs, the breaker trips and shuts off power.

main power wires · main power shutoff · hot bus bar · 240-volt breaker · 120-volt breaker · main neutral wire · neutral bus bar · system ground wire

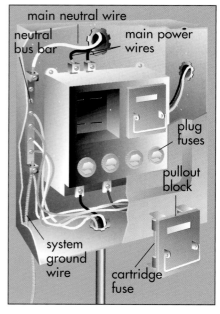

Don't substitute wrong size fuses.

Older homes have service panels with fuses rather than breakers. When an overload or short circuit occurs, a strip of wire breaks inside the fuse, shutting off power. If you have a overloaded circuit, do not replace a 15-amp with, say, a 20-amp fuse. Wiring that gets more current than it's designed for heats up and can cause a fire.

main neutral wire · neutral bus bar · main power wires · plug fuses · pullout block · system ground wire · cartridge fuse

CAUTION!

LEAVE INCOMING WIRES TO THE UTILITY COMPANY

If you suspect the wires entering your house may be damaged, do not touch them. Have the utility company inspect them. Usually, they'll do it at no charge.

GROUNDING ELECTRICAL CIRCUITS

Older homes may have ungrounded receptacles and fixtures; many local codes do not require rewiring these systems so they're grounded. However, grounding is a valuable protection against electrical shock. It provides a third path for electricity to travel along. If there is a short circuit, the electricity flows into the earth rather than into your body if you touch a defective fixture or outlet.

An electrical system is grounded by connecting it to a grounding rod driven 8 feet into the earth outside the house or to a cold-water pipe that enters the ground. Every branch circuit must be grounded as well, either with a separate wire leading to the neutral bar of the service panel or with metal sheathing running without a break from each outlet to the panel. In some areas, especially where the outlet and/or appliances may become wet, ground-fault circuit interrupter (GFCI) receptacles are required.

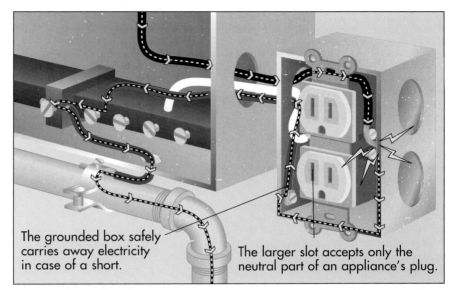

The grounded box safely carries away electricity in case of a short.

The larger slot accepts only the neutral part of an appliance's plug.

Use a polarized and grounded receptacle.

A polarized receptacle has one slot longer than the other. This ensures the plug is inserted so the hot current flows through hot wires and neutral current through white wires. Grounding offers a more effective protection against shock. The grounding circuit must follow an unbroken path to the earth.

The round hole in the receptacle is attached to metal conduit or sheathing that leads without interruption to the neutral bus bar of the main service panel. If your conduit or armored cable (BX) sheathing is not connected securely at all points or if your ground wire is disconnected, the circuit will not be grounded.

Map out your household circuits.

A well-planned electrical system, such as the one shown, has branch circuits serving easily defined areas or purposes. It is important that no circuit carries too great a load, or breakers or fuses will be constantly tripping or blowing. Some heavy-duty appliances require a circuit to themselves. The label on most appliances tells you how many amps it draws. If you only know the wattage of the unit, divide the wattage by 120 to determine amps. Add up the totals to make sure each circuit is not carrying more amps than it is designed for. For instance, a 15-amp circuit can handle a typical toaster (9 amps) and refrigerator (5 amps) and not much more. With receptacles, take into account the amperage of the appliances you plug into them.

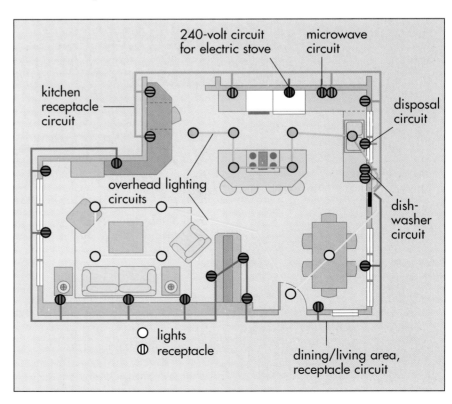

240-volt circuit for electric stove

microwave circuit

kitchen receptacle circuit

disposal circuit

overhead lighting circuits

dish-washer circuit

O lights
⑪ receptacle

dining/living area, receptacle circuit

CHOOSING ELECTRICAL CABLE AND BOXES

Wire is a solid strand of metal, usually encased in insulation. Cord is made of many small twisted strands, also encased in insulation. Cable is made of two or more wires wrapped in a protective metal or plastic sheath.

Most local building departments allow you to use nonmetallic (NM) sheathed cable inside walls, floors, and other places where it cannot be damaged or get wet. Install protective metal plates on the studs where cable passes through to ensure nails will not poke into the cable as you install drywall and trim.

Be sure to use the correct thickness, or gauge, of wire for your circuit: 14-gauge wire carries a maximum of 15 amps, 12-gauge carries up to 20 amps, and 10-gauge wire up to 30 amps.

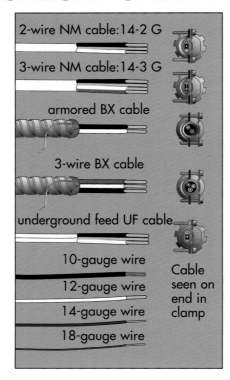

2-wire NM cable: 14-2 G
3-wire NM cable: 14-3 G
armored BX cable
3-wire BX cable
underground feed UF cable
10-gauge wire
12-gauge wire
14-gauge wire
18-gauge wire
Cable seen on end in clamp

Choose the cable or wire.
The top example has two 14-gauge wires plus a bare ground, so is labeled 14-2 G cable (G for ground). Cable marked 14-3 G has three wires plus a ground wire.

Flexible armored cable (BX) contains wires wrapped in a metal sheathing that acts as the ground. Rigid metal or flexible Greenfield conduit does not contain wire so you pull wires through the runs after it is installed.

Underground feed (UF) cable is watertight with the sheathing molded around the wire; it may be used in many areas for underground lines. Choose the clamp suitable for your cable. With BX, make sure the whole cable will fit. Doorbells and other low-voltage circuits typically use 18-gauge wire.

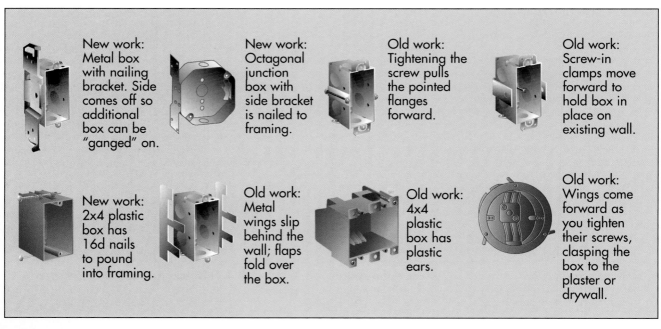

New work: Metal box with nailing bracket. Side comes off so additional box can be "ganged" on.

New work: Octagonal junction box with side bracket is nailed to framing.

Old work: Tightening the screw pulls the pointed flanges forward.

Old work: Screw-in clamps move forward to hold box in place on existing wall.

New work: 2x4 plastic box has 16d nails to pound into framing.

Old work: Metal wings slip behind the wall; flaps fold over the box.

Old work: 4x4 plastic box has plastic ears.

Old work: Wings come forward as you tighten their screws, clasping the box to the plaster or drywall.

Select boxes for new and old work.
All electrical connections and wire splices must be made inside approved electrical boxes. Every box must be accessible—never bury one in a wall. This protects your home from fire and makes future upgrades easier.

Boxes designed for new work—

where there is no existing wall surface—typically can be installed in a few seconds. Old-work or retrofit boxes take longer to install, but help you minimize damage to existing walls. Some metal boxes can be ganged together into double, triple, or larger boxes. Make sure your box will not be

overcrowded with wires—a dangerous situation. In fact, codes dictate how many wires can be in a certain-size box. For heavy chandeliers or ceiling fans, get a box that can be clamped firmly to joists. If you are using conduit or BX sheathing as your ground, you must use metal boxes.

WORKING WITH WIRE

D on't take shortcuts with wire connections and splices. A loose or imperfectly covered connection makes your home unsafe. Cap splices with wire connectors as well as with tape, and push connected wires carefully back into the electrical box. Instead of trying to connect two or more wires to a terminal, make pigtails wherever they are needed. Be careful not to overcrowd a box with too many wires. Stripping techniques are simple, but exercise care when removing sheathing so you don't damage the underlying insulation.

YOU'LL NEED
TIME: 5 minutes per connection.
SKILLS: Simple wire stripping.
TOOLS: Cable ripper or utility knife, lineman's pliers, wire strippers or combination tool.

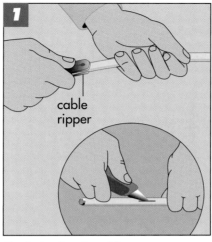

1. Strip the sheathing.
Using an inexpensive cable ripper, remove 6 to 8 inches of the plastic sheathing from a nonmetallic cable. Simply squeeze the cable ripper on the wire and pull. The same job can be done with a utility knife, but be careful to run the blade right down the middle so it doesn't strip the insulation from the wires.

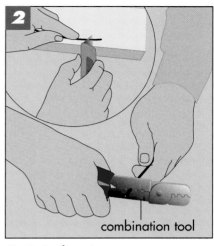

2. Strip the wire.
To strip wire with a combination tool, position the wire in the correct hole for the gauge of wire you're using. Clamp down, give it a twist, and pull off the insulation. If you use a utility knife, be careful not to dig into the copper wire. Place the wire on a scrap of wood, hold the blade at a slight angle, and make light slices.

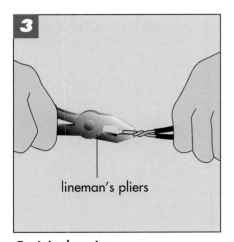

3. Join the wires.
To splice solid wires, cross them, grab both with lineman's pliers, and twist clockwise. Both wires should twist—don't just twist one wire around the other. Don't twist so tightly that the wires crack or break. To join a stranded wire to a solid wire, wrap the stranded wire around the solid wire, then bend the solid wire so it clamps down on the stranded wire.

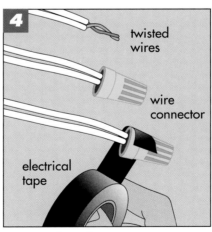

4. Cap the splice.
Choose the correct size of wire connectors; the package will tell you how many wires of which size they will accommodate. Twist the connector on by hand until it tightens firmly. Then wrap the connector and wires clockwise with electrical tape. Always twist wires together before using a connector—don't depend on the connector to do the joining.

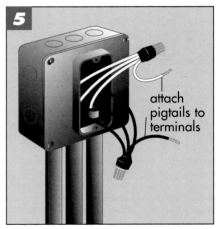

5. Add a pigtail when needed.
It is unsafe to connect two or more wires to a terminal of a switch, receptacle, or fixture. Their screws are made to hold only one wire. Cut a piece of wire about 4 inches long and strip both ends. Splice it to the other wires to form what electricians call a pigtail.

CONNECTING BOXES

If you are working with new construction, attaching electrical boxes to studs is simple. Many boxes come with built-in spacers and nails to help you position and attach them in a few seconds.

If you are remodeling, however, you have to deal with drywall or plaster already in place. The challenge is to install the boxes while damaging the walls as little as possible. Patching the walls likely will take far more time than installing the electrical boxes. Use special old-work boxes (see page 94) designed specifically for this type of work.

YOU'LL NEED

TIME: About 30 minutes a box, not including running new wire.
SKILLS: Measuring, cutting drywall or plaster.
TOOLS: Keyhole saw, screwdriver, needle-nose pliers, utility knife.

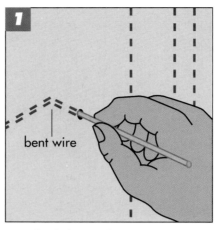

1. Check for studs.
Poke or drill a small hole in the wall. Insert a bent wire and rotate it. If you hit something, you've probably found a stud, so try a few inches to one side. If you strike wood again, you may have hit horizontal fire blocking. Try 3 inches higher or lower. Keep trying until you can rotate the bent wire freely.

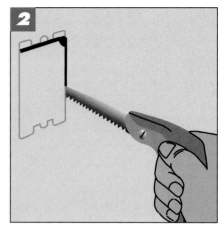

2. Cut the opening.
Hold the box against the wall, check for plumb, and trace around it to mark for your hole. If your wall surface is drywall, use a utility knife to cut through it. For plaster walls or to cut drywall quicker, use a keyhole saw. For a wood surface, drill a hole in each corner and make the cut with a sabersaw. Cut carefully to avoid having to patch the wall.

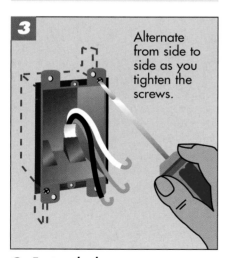

Alternate from side to side as you tighten the screws.

3. Fasten the box.
Run the cable to the opening (see page 97), pull 8 inches through an old-work box, and clamp it. The box shown above grips the wall from behind when you tighten the screws. Hold the box plumb as you tighten the screws, alternating from side to side so the box seats evenly. Other old-work boxes use wing clips or side flanges.

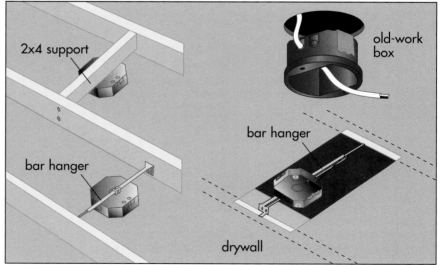

Install ceiling boxes.
If you have unfinished walls or if you can work from an attic space above, nail the box to a joist or attach a 2×4 support or special expandable bars to the joists. Then attach the box to these. If the walls are finished and your fixture is not heavy, use an old-work box. Cut and install it much as with the wall box shown above. For a heavy chandelier or a ceiling fan, cut out the drywall or plaster and install a bar hanger. If you cut carefully, you can reuse the drywall cutout when you patch the ceiling.

RUNNING CABLE

If you need to run cable in a finished space, begin by doing some detective work: Find out where the studs and joists are and whether there is insulation or fire blocking in the way. Make as few holes as possible as you probe the wall. Patching walls may be more work than running the wiring. You can run wire for short runs by simply poking the wire through the wall cavity. For long runs save yourself time and effort by buying a fish tape.

Whenever you drill, wear safety goggles and watch out for nails. Bore slowly to avoid burning out the drill.

YOU'LL NEED

TIME: Several hours per run.
SKILLS: Drilling and patching.
TOOLS: Drill, ¾- and 1-inch bits, fish tape, reciprocating or keyhole saw, utility knife, chisel, hammer.

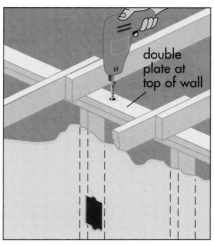

Fish cable from above.
If there is access from above or below, drill through the top or bottom plates of the wall frame. In awkward places, it often helps to have a bit extension. After drilling the hole, feed the cable to the box opening. If you hit fire blocking (horizontal pieces between studs), cut a small hole in the wall at that point and notch the blocking, as shown below left for studs.

Fish from below.
If there is no access above or below, cut an opening to expose the plate at the ceiling or floor. At the bottom, there will only be a single plate; remove the baseboard and make the cutout. Drill both holes using a bit extension. Have a helper tug the cable from another place while you feed it through the openings. Avoid kinks and damage to the sheathing.

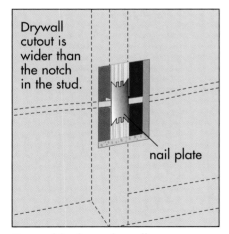

Run cable through walls.
If possible, remove baseboards or other moldings and run cable in the wall space behind them. This will save you wall patching. If you need to run cable horizontally in the middle of the wall, cut out rectangles at each stud and notch the stud with a chisel. Install a protective nail plate before you patch the wall.

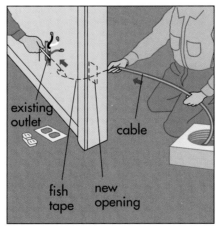

Fish cable from behind.
Thread one fish tape (or bent coat hanger) through one side, and another through the other. Wiggle them until they hook. Pull one tape through and attach the electrical cable to it by wrapping it with electrical tape. Then pull the cable through, strip and cut the cable, and make the connections.

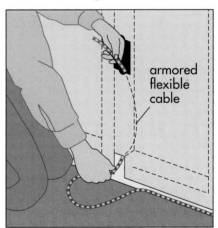

Run cable along baseboards.
To run cable behind baseboards, use armored flexible (BX) cable to avoid damage from nails. If the new opening is low enough, push the cable up to the opening. When going past doors, remove the casing and run the cable around the jamb opening. Take care when reattaching the molding; you can pierce armored cable with a nail.

INSTALLING OVERHEAD LIGHTING

There are hundreds of light fixtures to choose from, yet there are only a few methods of attaching them to electrical boxes. If you are replacing an existing fixture, chances are you can install the new one right on the old box without too much trouble.

To avoid extra trips to the store, check to make sure the hardware matches up. Also, inspect the old wires for cracked and discolored insulation due to excessive heat. This probably is a result of using a bulb that is higher in wattage than the manufacturer recommends. If the wire looks bad, strip it back to where it is sound.

YOU'LL NEED

TIME: About 1 hour to mount a simple fixture; more time for fans or elaborate units.
SKILLS: Basic electrical skills.
TOOLS: Screwdriver, pliers.

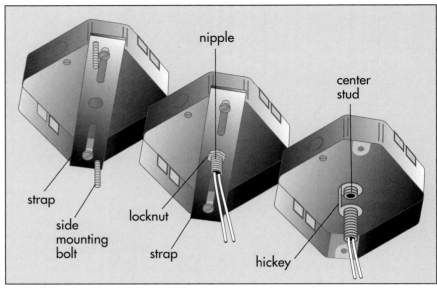

Select a mounting system.
If the screw or bolt holes in your fixture's canopy match those in the box, choose from the three mounting systems shown above. For fixtures with side mounting bolts, adapt by fastening a strap to the box. Some straps have several screw-in holes to choose from. For center-mounted fixtures, screw a nipple into the center hole of a strap and secure it in place with a locknut. If the box has a center stud, attaching a hickey is another way to adapt the box.

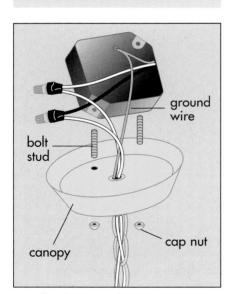

Install a hanging fixture.
Note: *Shut off the power.* Attach the canopy with a pair of bolt studs screwed directly into the box. Connect the wires and coil them up into the box. Push the canopy in place so the studs poke through the holes. Secure the canopy with cap nuts.

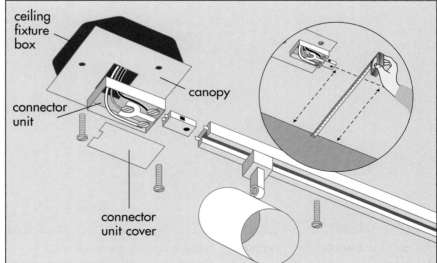

Install track lighting.
Note: *Shut off the power.* Attach the canopy using one of the mounting systems shown on this page above. Connect the wires from the fixture box to the connector unit. Install the connector unit to the canopy. Measure from the wall that is visually most important and draw layout lines for the tracks. Connect the track to the connector unit, then fasten it firmly to the ceiling. Snap on connector covers. Twist each light into place on the track. Use the manufacturer's instructions for specific installation details.

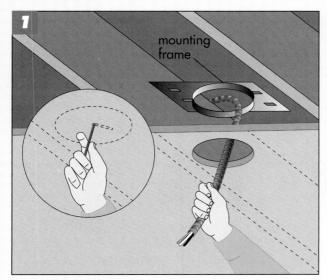

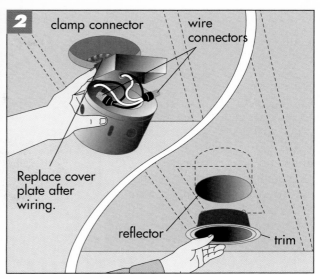

1. Install a recessed ceiling light.

Note: *Shut off the power.* Check for joists by drilling a hole and exploring with a bent wire (see inset). Then cut a hole in the ceiling using the template supplied by the manufacturer. Run cable, leaving an extra foot to work with. Strip 6 inches of sheathing and ¾ inch of insulation from the wires. Slip the mounting frame through the hole (it will just fit) and place it so the flange sits on the hole.

2. Wire and mount the fixture.

Remove the cover plate from the fixture's electrical box. Secure the cable to the box and connect the wires (see page 95). Push the wires into the box and reattach the cover plate. Slide the canister up through the mounting plate until it is recessed slightly, just above the ceiling surface. Secure it to the mounting plate with the screws provided. Fasten the reflector in place, screw in a bulb, and attach the trim.

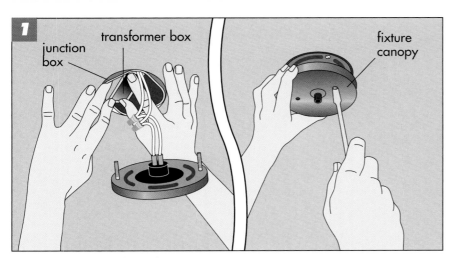

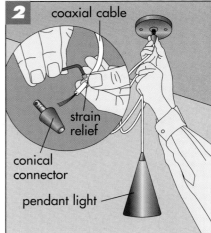

1. Install a low-voltage hanging light fixture.

Note: *Shut off the power.* Use an electrical junction box at the site of the light fixture. Connect the wires as you would for a hanging fixture (see page 98). Mount the transformer inside the box using the adhesive patches usually provided. Install the fixture canopy as you would with a standard fixture. Decide how far down you want the pendant light to hang and add 1¼ inches. Cut the coaxial cable and strip off 1¼ inches of the outer wrap. Strip ½ inch of plastic insulation from the inner wire of the coaxial cable. Feed the coaxial cable into the bottom of the conical connector.

2. Adjust cable, attach light.

With an Allen wrench, fasten the strain relief on the cable so it overlaps the stripped end of the outer wrap. Follow manufacturer's instructions to be sure the cable is seated. Tighten the Allen screw that grips the strain relief inside the conical connector. Screw the conical connector into the canopy. Insert the light bulb.

WALLS

Turning damaged walls into smooth, pleasing surfaces can be a time-consuming job, especially if you have old plaster walls. There is no magic substance to straighten things out quickly. A new coat of paint, or even most wallpapers, will not cover up imperfections. In fact, such coverings actually may accentuate the cracks and bumps on a wall.

For both plaster and drywall surfaces, test the integrity of the wall by pushing on it at many points. If the drywall or plaster is spongy, you need to patch the area or cracks will reappear.

Some homes—most often, those built since the 1960s—have ceilings with machine-blown texture material that looks like cottage cheese. Special materials are available for patching these surfaces, but it is difficult to achieve an exact match. For the best results, hire a contractor to redo the whole ceiling. Or, remove the texture by wetting it with a mister and scraping it off with a 6-inch taping blade.

WALL REPAIR CHART

PROBLEM	SOLUTION
Hole in drywall or plaster	Cut out damaged area and install a drywall patch (see page 101).
Hairline cracks in plaster	If the plaster is not spongy, spray with an aerosol crack patcher, prime, and paint.
Large cracks in plaster	If the plaster is not spongy, key the crack (see page 101) and apply joint compound. Or, apply mesh tape and cover with joint compound, feathering it out each side at least 6 inches.
Loose, spongy plaster	For small sections, chop out the loose material, screw pieces of drywall in the hole, and tape. For large sections, either remove the plaster and drywall, or skin over the plaster with drywall. Remove moldings first, then install small strips of wood to make up for the thickness of the drywall before reattaching the moldings.
Cracks in drywall	Apply mesh tape and joint compound, feathering it out at least 6 inches on either side of the tape.
Peeling or alligator-skinned paint	This can be a real headache. If you cannot scrape off the paint completely, you must apply new drywall for a smooth surface. Or, make a textured surface using joint compound mixed with a little sand and water.
Nailheads popping up in drywall.	Remove the nail and pound a new one firmly into a stud.
Drywall tape peeling	Remove the tape, then apply new tape and joint compound.

MATERIALS TO USE

MATERIAL	USES
Spackle	Dries quickly but is soft. Use only for filling small holes shortly before painting.
Ready-mixed joint compound	Quick to use because there is no mixing; sands easily. Will take a long time to dry if laid on thick and/or if conditions are humid; a fan will speed up drying time considerably. Strong enough for covering drywall tape, but not recommended as a first coat for repairs or places where you need to fill in holes.
Dry-mix joint compound	Comes in bags marked 20, 45, or 90. These numbers roughly tell you how many minutes you have before the mix sets. So 90 is the best choice unless you have only a small place to repair. Strong but hard to sand. Use as a first coat for drywall or repairs.
Perlited gypsum (plaster)	Use for filling in large or thick holes; mix this with dry-mix joint compound for a substance that will not sag.
Caulk	Not generally recommended. But if you use a high-quality caulk (latex/silicone is a good choice), it can fill in cracks quickly and may last for years because it is flexible. Smooth with your finger and then a damp rag immediately after applying.

REPAIRING DRYWALL AND PLASTER

Before repairing a hole or crack in drywall, check the surrounding area for sponginess. If it is spongy, repair that area as well (see chart on page 100). If you need to patch a large area, fill it in with a piece of drywall first. Make sure the drywall is not thicker than the plaster. Attach the patch with screws rather than nails so you do not shake the wall, loosening more plaster. Prime the patches before painting to ensure you achieve a consistent color.

YOU'LL NEED

TIME: About 1 hour to make the patch and apply the first coat of compound. Budget time for several coats with a half day of drying between.
SKILLS: You can learn to patch effectively in a day or so.
TOOLS: Utility knife, taping knives, screwdriver or drill, old-fashioned can opener.

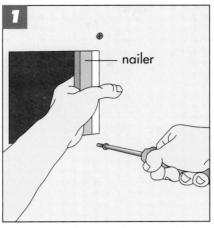

1. Cut out damaged area and anchor a nailer.
Remove all loose, cracked, or softened wall material. Cut a patch, place it over the hole, trace around it, and cut out an opening. Attach nailers behind the wall by driving screws through the drywall and into the nailers. For plaster walls, you simply may be able to stuff the hole with wadded-up newspaper before applying joint compound.

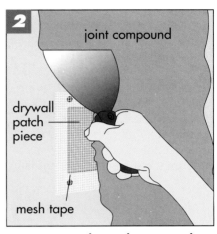

2. Insert patch, apply tape and joint compound.
Fill in the hole with a piece of drywall. It does not have to be exact. Make sure it is not too thick or it will protrude from the wall surface. Cut small pieces of mesh tape to fit and press them in place. Apply joint compound, covering the tape and feathering it out at least 6 inches on all sides. Allow it to dry, apply two or more coats, and sand smooth.

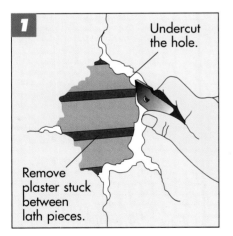

1. Key plaster before patching.
Undercut the plaster so the back edge of the hole is larger than the top. This "keys" the patching material into the wall. An older type of pointed can opener works well for this job or use a chisel. Remove plaster stuck between the cracks of the lath. These spaces also give the new material something to grab onto.

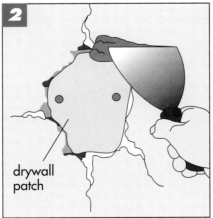

2. Fill a plaster hole.
Fill in large cavities with drywall. Make sure it is not thicker than the plaster. For small holes just use patching material. Combine dry-mix joint compound with perlited gypsum in a 50/50 mix. Add water to make a firm consistency. Apply it with a wide taping knife. For subsequent coats, use ready-mix drywall compound.

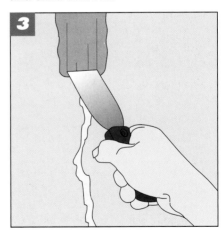

3. Patch a crack in plaster.
Patch cracks with joint compound. Scratch the cracks with a knife or old-fashioned can opener to make a V shape so the compound will adhere better. Force the material tightly into the crack. Repeat with several coats and sand smooth. Or, apply mesh tape and feather out both sides when you apply the joint compound.

WORKING WITH DRYWALL

Drywall is inexpensive, and hanging techniques are easy to learn. However, installing drywall is difficult work. The sheets are heavy and unwieldy. Many older rooms are out of square, so cutting often is difficult. Finishing to a smooth surface takes three applications and sandings even for professionals—you should expect four or five.

Before you hang drywall, study your framing to make sure you will be able to attach the drywall at all points. If you are covering over an existing wall, locate all the joists and studs and clearly mark their locations on the walls, ceilings, or floors.

YOU'LL NEED

TIME: With a helper, a day to hang a medium-sized room.
SKILLS: Measuring, careful lifting.
TOOLS: Tape measure, drywall square, utility knife, drywall saw, chalk line, hammer, drywall taping blades.

Trap square with foot.

Cut backing after breaking.

1. Make a crosscut.

Lay the drywall sheets on top of 1× or 2× scrap lumber to hold them up off the floor. Before you cut, you may have to turn over some pieces so the finished side is facing you. Mark the sheet ¼ inch shorter than the measured length. Stand the drywall on edge and set your drywall square in place.

Clasp the square firmly on top and press your foot against the bottom of the square's blade to make sure it doesn't move. With the blade against the square, cut downward most of the way, then finish by cutting up from the bottom. Snap the cut segment back away from the cut, then cut through the backing paper.

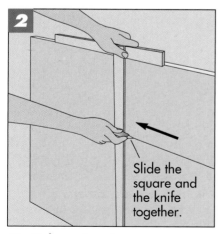

Slide the square and the knife together.

2. Make a rip cut.

To make a cut along the length of a piece of drywall, set the drywall square on the edge of a sheet, and hold the knife against it at the correct spot. Slide the square along as you keep the knife in position. If the rip cut must be wider at one end, chalk a line and cut freehand.

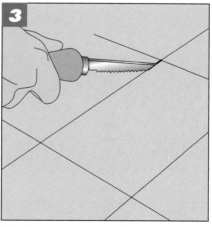

3. Cut out a rectangle.

To make a hole for a receptacle box, measure from the box's edges, top, and bottom to the edges of the adjacent sheets. Transfer the measurements to the sheet and draw a rectangle. Score the surface with a utility knife and cut out the hole with a drywall saw.

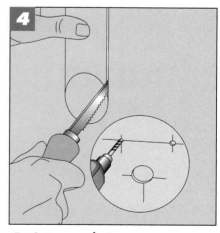

4. Cut around pipes.

To cut a hole for a pipe, measure and mark the sheet for the center of the pipe. Then draw a circle, and cut it out with a drywall saw or a knife. Or, you can drill a hole, using a holesaw slightly larger than the pipe's diameter. Bore small holes with a power drill.

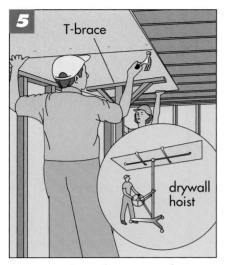

5. Hang the ceiling pieces first.

Start in a corner, keeping the panels perpendicular to the joists. Mark the locations of the joists on the sheet before you hoist it up. Searching for joists while holding it up can be frustrating. Construct one or two braces of 2×4s to hold the panels temporarily in place or rent a drywall hoist.

6. Hang wall sheets.

To install sheets horizontally, butt the upper sheets firmly against the ceiling drywall. Cut sheets so they fall midway across a stud. Butt the lower panels firmly against the upper panels, tapered edge to tapered edge. When covering existing plaster, apply adhesive and drive screws into the lath only at the edges of the drywall.

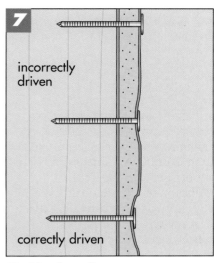

7. Dimple nails.

Drive in nails so they form a dimple that can be filled with joint compound. Do not break the paper, or the nail will lose its holding power. If you are attaching drywall with screws, use a dimpler bit and take care to drive the screws straight rather than at an angle.

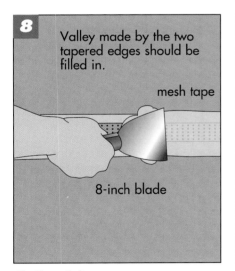

8. Tape joints.

Press mesh tape in place. Load an 8- or 10-inch blade with joint compound. Make sure the blade more than spans the valley created by the tapers. Fill in the taper only, so there is a flat wall surface. For butt joints, feather out compound 8 to 10 inches on each side. If you end up with a small ridge in the middle, you can sand it off after the compound dries.

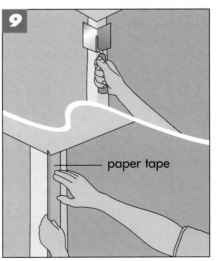

9. Tape inside corners.

Apply compound to both sides with a 6-inch blade. Cut a piece of paper tape, fold it along its crease, and pat it into the corner. Keep it straight to avoid wrinkles. Run a corner blade down its length to embed the tape. Lift the tape and add compound where tape doesn't adhere. On the first coat, make a straight line at the corner; feather later coats with a 10-inch blade.

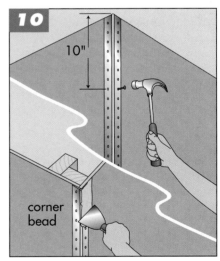

10. Tape outside corners.

Cut metal corner bead to fit using tin snips. Fasten it to the walls with nails or screws at 10-inch intervals. Be sure the flange does not stick out at any point. Test for this by running a taping blade along the bead's length. When applying joint compound, let the blade ride on the bead. Use a 6-inch blade for the first coat, then 10- and 12-inch blades.

FLOORS

Before you can install new flooring, the surface must be prepared for the particular material you will be using. First, check for serious dips, slants, or high spots using a long, straight board and a level. Any depression or bump over ¾ inch in an average-sized kitchen usually will be visible under the new flooring. To solve this problem, you may be able to jack up a post in the basement—a big job. It may be easier to level the floor with new underlayment.

Avoid situations where the new floor abuts a floor surface ¾ inch or more higher, creating a slight step up at the place where the floors meet. This is hazardous and looks unprofessional as well. You may need to remove a layer or two of old flooring to achieve a smooth transition between the surfaces.

For vinyl tile or sheet goods, the surface must be perfectly smooth. Any imperfections will show through in time. If you want to lay such flooring over old tiles that have an embossed pattern, use embossing leveler to smooth out the pattern. Often, the easiest solution is to install underlayment.

Ceramic tile requires a strong base. When you jump on the floor, you should not feel the floor flex. If you do, you may need to take out the old subflooring and replace it with plywood. If you have access from below, consider adding diagonal bridging between joists to shore up the floor.

YOU'LL NEED

TIME: About a day to install a subfloor in an average kitchen.
SKILLS: Measuring and cutting plywood, fastening with screws or nails.
TOOLS: Flat pry bar, circular saw, hand saw, hammer, drill, carpenter's square, chalk line.

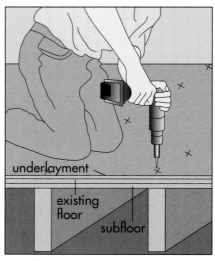

Install underlayment.
Often, the easiest way to achieve a smooth surface is to apply a layer of ¼-inch plywood. Buy 4×4 sheets of underlayment with Xs printed on them to show where to drive in nails or screws in a grid pattern. Start at a square corner and, if possible, lay several sheets in place before you start fastening.

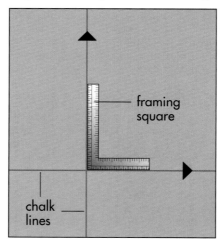

Draw a layout for the tiles.
Take time to lay out a plan for the tile. Measure from the most visible wall or fixture to make sure this line will be straight. If you have several visible lines fairly close to each other that are not square or parallel to each other (as often happens in a bathroom), plan a layout that splits the difference.

Undercut molding.
When you are confronted with door casings or other moldings that make for awkard cuts, use a handsaw to cut the molding high enough to slide the finished flooring under it. Use flooring patch or leveler to fill in gaps or holes, then sand it smooth.

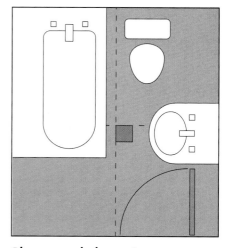

Plan around obstructions.
Avoid having small tile pieces between fixtures. You may have to start with three-quarter-sized pieces to do this. Wide tiles that are not parallel to a wall or fixture will not look as bad as narrow tiles. Mark chalk lines square to each other; locating the intersection where it makes sense for you to start tiling.

INSTALLING VINYL TILES

Commercial tiles that are ⅛ inch thick will cover up some minor floor imperfections. However, even the tiniest bump will show through thin tiles with glossy surfaces. Some tiles need to be installed in a particular direction; there will be arrows printed on their backs. Self-adhesive tiles cannot be guaranteed to stay put, so apply clear adhesive to the floor before laying them. Work as neatly as possible, wiping away excess adhesive as you go and keeping your hands clean. Remove the base shoe carefully and reinstall it after laying the tiles.

YOU'LL NEED

TIME: Half a day for a kitchen.
SKILLS: Measuring and cutting.
TOOLS: Utility knife, tape measure, notched trowel.

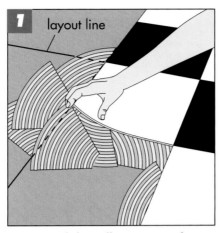

1. Trowel the adhesive, set tiles.
In a regular pattern, apply adhesive with a thin-notched trowel. Allow the adhesive to dry to the touch. Lay the first tiles in a pyramid, taking care to stay on the layout lines. Don't slide tile into place. Instead, butt each tile to the adjacent tiles.

2. Trim tiles to fit.
To measure for cuts, lay one tile squarely on top of the last full tile. Then lay another one on top of it, flush against the wall, and mark the lower tile. To mark for a corner, mark the tile from both walls, being careful not to rotate the tile to be cut.

INSTALLING SHEET FLOORING

Work methodically and carefully with sheet goods because if you make one mistake, the whole sheet will need to be replaced. Choose sheet goods that come with an equal-sized piece of thick paper you can use for a template. Or, use construction paper to make your own template. Avoid seams; even when installed by a professional, seams can come apart after a few years. Remove base shoes and molding. Install threshold pieces so you will not have to cut the sheet perfectly. If flooring a bathroom, remove the toilet and pedestal sink.

YOU'LL NEED

TIME: A full day for an average kitchen or bathroom.
SKILLS: Careful measuring and cutting.
TOOLS: Knife, tape measure, paint brush for applying adhesive.

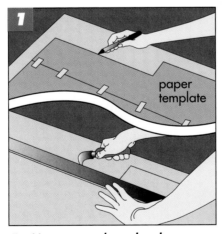

1. Measure and cut the sheet.
Unroll the uncut sheet goods in another room to flatten out and come to room temperature. Make a template by laying a large sheet of paper on the floor and cutting it to fit. When the whole thing fits, lay the template on the flooring sheet. Tape it to make sure it doesn't move, mark its outline with a pencil, and cut the sheet with a knife or pair of shears.

2. Glue the sheet down.
Position the sheet on the floor, checking to make sure it doesn't need trimming. Picking up one section at a time, brush on the adhesive around the perimeter of the room. Press the sheet into place, then replace the base shoe, threshold, and any fixtures or cabinets you removed. Make sure there are no edges of the flooring that are not protected by trim.

INSTALLING CERAMIC FLOOR TILE

Ceramic tile is a good choice for a kitchen or bathroom where water may get on the floor. Buy the adhesive along with the tiles to make sure you get the right kind. Usually, a thinset mortar works best. Choose a grout whose color is similar to the tiles. Determine how wide you want the grout lines to be and purchase plastic spacers. Be sure the subfloor is strong. If it flexes at all, the grout or the tiles can crack.

YOU'LL NEED

TIME: About 1 day to lay an average kitchen or bathroom; several hours to grout it on the following day.
SKILLS: Measuring, cutting with a tile cutter.
TOOLS: Tile cutter, nibbling tool, tape measure, grout float, beater board, hammer or rubber mallet.

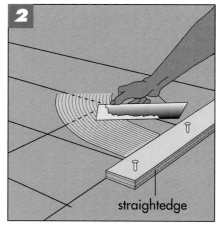

1. Prepare the floor.
If you are not sure whether your wood subfloor is strong enough, call in a professional. Make sure the adhesive will stick to the existing floor; you may need to remove a layer of flooring. To lay out the room (see page 104), set the tiles in a dry run with spacers to make sure you don't end up with narrow pieces along one wall.

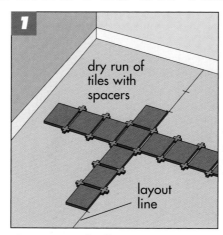

2. Set straightedge, trowel.
Anchor a long, perfectly straight board along what will be the most visible line of tiles. (The factory edge of a piece of plywood works well.) With the correct size of notched trowel, spread mortar on about 4 square feet, troweling it smooth and level with the notches. Make sure you can see the layout lines through the troweled mortar.

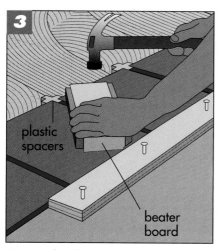

3. Set the tiles.
Press one edge of the first tiles against the straightedge, and use the layout lines to align them in the other directions. Place the plastic spacers at tile corners as you work to maintain even grout lines. To ensure the tiles are all on the same level and they adhere fully to the adhesive, set them with a beater board.

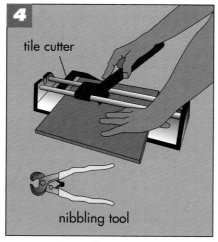

4. Cut tiles to fit.
Measure for cutting using the technique shown on page 105. For straight cuts, use a tile cutter, as shown. To trim pieces to go around outside corners, use a nibbling tool or a circular saw with a masonry cutting blade. If you have many cutouts to make or if you use a material that a tile cutter cannot cut, such as marble, rent a wet saw designed for tile.

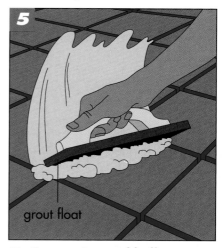

5. Grout, wipe, and buff.
Mix the grout according to directions, using a latex additive if needed. With a grout float, push the grout into the joints, then press with a wiping motion in at least two directions. Finish by tilting the float up to remove the excess grout. Wipe the surface with a large, wet towel to clean the tiles. Once dry, buff with a cloth.

LAYING LAMINATE STRIP FLOORING

Laminate strip flooring adds the warmth of wood to any room in which you install it. This material is easy to install and has a strong, scratch-resistant surface. Begin with a fairly smooth, level floor. You also can purchase foam underlayment to absorb sound. If you install strip flooring on concrete, first apply a polyethylene film as a vapor barrier. Remove any base shoe; you can reuse it or purchase a base shoe to match the new flooring.

To make your room appear more spacious, run the planks along the length of the room rather than the width.

YOU'LL NEED

TIME: Most of a day for an average size kitchen floor.
SKILLS: Measuring, cutting.
TOOLS: Circular saw, hammer, tape measure.

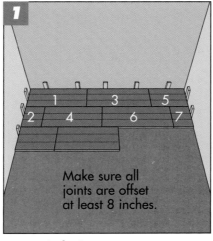

Make sure all joints are offset at least 8 inches.

1. Begin laying out.

Lay the first two rows in place without gluing. Use spacers to keep the planks ⅛ to ¼ inch away from all walls. Cut the boards face-side-down to avoid chipping them. Do not use pieces on the ends that are less than 8 inches long. Once you have the pieces in place, you may have to cut some of them lengthwise. Glue the pieces in the order shown above.

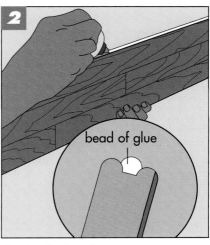

bead of glue

2. Apply the glue.

Wherever one plank joins another plank, apply glue to the groove. Glue both the long and short sides. Don't apply glue to grooves that meet against a wall. Be sure to fill the entire groove with glue, then wipe away the excess after you install them.

Install the first two rows, then wait an hour before installing the rest of the floor.

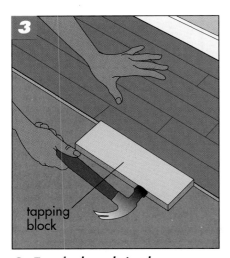

tapping block

3. Tap the boards in place.

Glue the grooves and push each plank into position. With a scrap piece of wood, tap them together tightly. Never hit the plank itself with a hammer. Wipe away all excess glue with a damp cloth. Make sure each joint is tight before moving on. You won't be able to fix the joints later.

scrap piece of flooring

4. Cut the last row.

To mark the last row for cutting, cut the pieces to length and place them exactly on top of the the last installed row. With a full-width scrap of the flooring, trace the cut line by dragging the scrap and a pencil, as shown. Cut the row narrow enough so there will be a gap of ⅛ to ¼ inch along the wall.

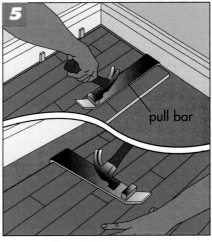

pull bar

5. Use the pull bar.

In places where you don't have room to swing a hammer, a special pull bar comes in handy. With it, you can tap the pieces tight without marring the wood.

Go over the floor with a damp rag to remove all excess glue. Allow the glue to dry overnight before using the floor.

GLOSSARY

If you are puzzled occasionally by remodeling terminology, these definitions should help. For words not listed here or for more about those that are, refer to the index, pages 110–112.

Access panel. A removable panel in a tub surround, wall, or ceiling that permits repair or replacement of concealed items, such as whirlpool pumps or faucet bodies.

Actual dimension. The true size of a piece of lumber, after milling and drying. See *nominal dimension.*

Amp (A). A measurement of the amount of electrical current in a circuit at any moment. See *Volt* and *Watt.*

Ballcock. The assembly inside a toilet tank that when activated releases water into the bowl to start the flushing action, then prepares the toilet for subsequent flushes. Also called a flush valve.

Batt. A section of fiberglass or rock-wool insulation measuring 15 or 23 inches wide by 4 to 8 feet long.

Bearing wall. An interior or exterior wall that helps support the roof or the floor joists above.

Box. A metal or plastic enclosure within which electrical connections are made.

Building codes. Community ordinances governing the manner in which a home or other structure may be constructed or modified. Most codes deal primarily with fire and health concerns and have separate sections relating to electrical, plumbing, and structural work.

Cable. Two or more insulated conductors wrapped in metal or plastic sheathing.

Casing. Trim work around a door, window, or other opening.

Caulk. Any of a variety of different compounds used to seal seams and joints against infiltration of water and air.

Circuit. The path of electrical flow from a power source through an outlet and back to ground.

Circuit breaker. A switch that automatically interrupts electrical flow in a circuit in case of an overload or short.

Closet bend. The elbow-shaped fitting beneath toilets that carries waste to the main drain.

Conduit. Rigid or flexible tubing through which wires are run.

Corner bead. Lightweight, perforated metal angle used to reinforce outside corners in drywall construction.

Countersink. To drive the head of a nail or screw so its top is flush with the surface of the surrounding wood.

Dimension lumber. A piece of lumber 2 inches or more thick and at least 2 inches wide.

Drain-waste-vent (DWV) system. The network of pipes carrying liquid and solid wastes out of a building and to a public sewer, a septic tank, or a cesspool and allowing for passage of sewer gases to the outside air.

Drywall. A basic interior building material consisting of sheets of pressed gypsum faced with heavy paper on both sides. Also known as gypsum board, plasterboard, and Sheetrock (a trade name).

Edging. Strips of wood or veneer used to cover the edges of plywood or boards.

Fish tape. A long strip of spring steel used for pulling cables and wires through conduit or walls.

Furring. Lightweight wood or metal strips used to even up a wall or ceiling for paneling or drywall. On masonry, furring provides a surface on which to nail.

Fuse. A safety device designed to stop electrical flow if a circuit shorts or is overloaded. Like a circuit breaker, it protects against fire from overheated wiring.

General-purpose circuit. A electrical circuit serving several light and/or receptacle outlets. See *Heavy-duty circuit* and *Small appliance circuit.*

Ground. An object that directs electricity through the shortest possible path to the earth. Neutral wires carry electricity to ground in all circuits. An additional grounding wire, or the sheathing of metal-clad cable or conduit, protects against shock from a malfunctioning device.

Ground-fault circuit interrupter (GFCI). A safety device that senses any shock hazard and shuts down a circuit or receptacle.

Grout. A thin mortar mixture. (See *mortar.*)

Heavy-duty circuit. An electrical circuit serving one 120- to 240-volt appliance See *General-purpose circuit* and *Small-appliance circuit.*

Hot wire. The electrical conductor that carries current to a receptacle or other outlet. See *Ground* and *Neutral wire*.

Jamb. The top and side frames of a door or window opening.

Joint compound. A synthetic-based formula used to conceal joints between drywall panels.

Joists. Horizontal framing members that support a floor and/or ceiling.

Kilowatt (kw). One thousand watts. A kilowatt hour is the standard measure of electrical consumption.

Laminate. A hard, plastic decorative veneer applied to cabinets and shelves.

Level. The condition that exists when any type of surface is at true horizontal. Also a tool used to determine level.

Miter joint. The joint formed when two members meet that have been cut at the same angle, usually 45 degrees.

Molding. A strip of wood, usually small-dimensioned, used to cover exposed edges or as decoration.

Mortar. A mixture of masonry cement, masonry sand, and water. For most jobs, the proportion of cement to sand is 1:3.

Neutral wire. The electrical conductor that carries current from an outlet back to ground. It is clad in white insulation. See *Ground* and *Hot wire*.

Nominal dimension. The stated size of a piece of lumber, such as a 2×4 or a 1×12. The actual dimension is somewhat smaller.

Outlet. Any potential point of use in a circuit, including receptacles, switches, and light fixtures.

Particleboard. Panels made from compressed wood chips and glue.

Partition. An interior dividing wall. Partitions may or may not be load bearing.

Plumb. The condition that exists when a member is at true vertical.

Receptacle. An electrical outlet that supplies power for lamps and other plug-in devices.

Roughing-in. The process of preparing the initial stage of a plumbing, electrical, carpentry, or other project, when all components that won't be seen after the second finishing phase are assembled.

Service panel. The main fuse or breaker box in a home.

Shim. A thin strip or wedge of wood or other material used to fill a gap between two adjoining components or to help establish level or plumb.

Small-appliance circuit. An electrical circuit that usually only has two or three 20-amp receptacle outlets.

Soil stack. A vertical drainpipe that carries wastes toward the sewer drain. The main soil stack is the largest vertical drain line of a building into which liquid and solid wastes from branch drains flow. See also *vent stack*.

Square. The condition that exists when one surface is at a 90-degree angle to another. Also a tool used to determine square.

Stop valve. A device installed in a water supply line, usually near a fixture, that lets you shut off the water supply to one fixture without interrupting service to the rest of the system.

Studs. Vertical 2×4 or 2×6 framing members spaced at regular intervals within a wall.

Taping. The process of covering drywall joints with paper or mesh tape and joint compound.

Template. A pattern cut from wood, paper, or other material that serves as a guide for certain cutting tools.

Toenail. To drive a nail at an angle, so as to hold together two pieces of material.

Trap. The part of a fixture drain that creates a water seal to prevent sewer gases from penetrating a home's interior. Codes require that all fixtures be trapped.

Vent stack. The upper portion of a vertical drain line through which gases pass directly to the outside. The main vent stack is the portion of the main vertical drain line above the highest fixture connected to it through which sewer gases from various fixtures escape upward and to the outside.

Volt (V). A measure of electrical pressure. See *Amp, Watt*.

Watt (W). A measure of the power an electrical device consumes. Watts = volts × amps. See *Amp, Kilowatt,* and *Volt*.

Wet wall. A strategically place cavity (usually a 2×6 wall) in which the main drain/vent stack and a cluster of supply and drain-waste-vent lines are housed.

Zoning. Ordinances regulating the ways in which a property may be used in a given neighborhood.

INDEX

METRIC CONVERSIONS

U.S. UNITS TO METRIC EQUIVALENTS			METRIC UNITS TO U.S. EQUIVALENTS		
To Convert From	Multiply By	To Get	To Convert From	Multiply By	To Get
Inches	25.4	Millimeters	Millimeters	0.0394	Inches
Inches	2.54	Centimeters	Centimeters	0.3937	Inches
Feet	30.48	Centimeters	Centimeters	0.0328	Feet
Feet	0.3048	Meters	Meters	3.2808	Feet
Yards	0.9144	Meters	Meters	1.0936	Yards
Miles	1.6093	Kilometers	Kilometers	0.6214	Miles
Square inches	6.4516	Square centimeters	Square centimeters	0.1550	Square inches
Square feet	0.0929	Square meters	Square meters	10.764	Square feet
Square yards	0.8361	Square meters	Square meters	1.1960	Square yards
Acres	0.4047	Hectares	Hectares	2.4711	Acres
Square miles	2.5899	Square kilometers	Square kilometers	0.3861	Square miles
Cubic inches	16.387	Cubic centimeters	Cubic centimeters	0.0610	Cubic inches
Cubic feet	0.0283	Cubic meters	Cubic meters	35.315	Cubic feet
Cubic feet	28.316	Liters	Liters	0.0353	Cubic feet
Cubic yards	0.7646	Cubic meters	Cubic meters	1.3079	Cubic yards
Cubic yards	764.55	Liters	Liters	0.0013	Cubic yards
Fluid ounces	29.574	Milliliters	Milliliters	0.0338	Fluid ounces
Quarts	0.9464	Liters	Liters	1.0567	Quarts
Gallons	3.7854	Liters	Liters	0.2642	Gallons
Drams	1.7718	Grams	Grams	0.5644	Drams
Ounces	28.350	Grams	Grams	0.0353	Ounces
Pounds	0.4536	Kilograms	Kilograms	2.2046	Pounds

To convert from degrees Fahrenheit (°F) to degrees Celsius (°C), first subtract 32, then multiply by ⁵⁄₉ (0.5555).

To convert from degrees Celsius (°C) to degrees Fahrenheit (°F), multiply by ⁹⁄₅ (1.8) then add 32.